John L. (John Lawrence) LeConte

Synopsis of the Lampyridae of the United States

John L. (John Lawrence) LeConte

Synopsis of the Lampyridae of the United States

ISBN/EAN: 9783741129834

Manufactured in Europe, USA, Canada, Australia, Japa

Cover: Foto ©Thomas Meinert / pixelio.de

Manufactured and distributed by brebook publishing software
(www.brebook.com)

John L. (John Lawrence) LeConte

Synopsis of the Lampyridae of the United States

Synopsis of the LAMPYRIDÆ of the United States.

BY JOHN L. LECONTE, M. D.

The term Lampyridæ in this memoir is used in the same extended sense as in my work on Classification of Coleoptera of North America. The species may be naturally divided into three sub-families of equal value, as follows:

Middle coxæ contiguous; epipleuræ distinct..2.
Middle coxæ distant; epipleuræ wanting..I. LYCIDÆ.
2.—Episterna of metathorax sinuate on inner side; epipleuræ usually wide at the base.. ....II. LAMPYRIDÆ.
Episterna of metathorax not sinuate on inner side; epipleuræ narrow at base.......................... ....III. TELEPHORIDÆ.

The relations of these and their respective tribes have already been sufficiently indicated by me in other places* in a condensed manner, and additional remarks will be found below under the appropriate headings.

Since publishing the popular essay on Lightning bugs above cited, my attention has been called by a friend, more familiar than myself with the literature of physical research to an interesting essay by Dr. T. L. Phipson,† in which some partially successful attempts were made to isolate the light giving substance, to which the name Noctilucine was applied. Other memoirs on this substance are cited by Dr. Phipson, but notice of them would unduly extend the present remarks.‡

If Dr. Phipson is correct in stating that the cause of luminosity both in living animals of such varied grades as the lower marine forms of life, the myriapoda and the complex terrestrial insects, and in the decomposing masses of animal and vegetable material such as foxfire and putrid fish is identical, these phenomena become even more worthy of careful study than I supposed when I wrote my popular essay on Lightning bugs. For a substance which is developed not only by normal physiological processes, in the bodies of animals of very varied structure, but by the somewhat fortuitous processes of ordinary putrifaction should certainly be within easy reach of synthesis.

---

* Canadian Entomologist, 1880, 174–184. Conf. Class. Col. N. America, 182–190.

† British Association for the Advancement of Science, Bristol, 1875; reprinted in Journal of the Franklin Institute, Philadelphia, January, 1876, 68.

‡ Phipson, sur la Noctilucine, Comptes Rendus, August 26, 1872, p. 547; Robin et Lalboulene, ibid. August 25, 1873.

Dr. Phipson also states that the spectroscopic examination of the light from these varied sources is contained within the space extending from C to a little beyond F, "but its brightest portion lies between E and F, and in most cases this portion only is visible, and the light appears nearly monochromatic. It has no lines nor bands of absorption."

There are several remarkable phenomena exhibited in various parts of the family which will receive more attention when the materials have been collected, and the student found to prepare a general monograph. They may be briefly stated as follows, for the purpose of guiding observations:

1. The pupæ of the Lycidæ are frequently found in large numbers, under loose pieces of bark, suspended closely together by the posterior extremity, each one enveloped in its own larva skin, which is cleft on the pleural lines as usual. Nothing of this kind has been observed in the other two sub-families.

2. The elytra of certain Lycidæ, though useless in flight, are expanded to a degree unknown in any other Coleopterous family.

3. The sexual differences in the light organs of various genera of Lampyridæ have not been properly recorded. They furnish as will be seen in the sequel, good generic and even specific characters.

4. The enormous vegetative development of the antennal branches in *Phengodes*, and the entire want of knowledge of the females of any member of the tribe.

5. The investigation of the relation between the Phengodini of this continent and the Drilini of other regions, with a view to the possible union of the two tribes.

6. While in the Phengodini we have an enormous development of antennal surface, we have in *Malthodes*, probably the lowest form in the family, an equally remarkable growth of the sexual appendages of the male.

Telephoridæ have occurred in tertiary strata;* the geological history of the other two sub-families is unknown.

Sub-family I.—LYCIDÆ.

The species of this sub-family are diurnal in habits and are found on the leaves of plants, where they seek their insect food.

They are known by the middle coxæ being rather widely separated by the mesosternum, and by the epipleuræ being reduced to a narrow thickened marginal line. Besides these essential characters of defini-

* Heer, Insecten fauna . . . Œningen & Radoboj, 143.

tion, other characters are seen in these insects not found in the other sub-families.

The elytra are frequently costate and coarsely reticulate with fine elevated lines forming a coarse net work, or more usually a regularly goffered surface. The head is sometimes prolonged in front of the eyes into a long narrow beak, which in other species becomes broad and short and in many of the species entirely disappears. The mandibles are feeble, slender and acute, the palpi are unequal and the eyes larger in the ♂ than ♀, though never very large; they are widely separated above and beneath. The antennæ are eleven-jointed, but the second joint is sometimes very short and inconspicuous; they are frequently very broad and compressed, and the joints 3—10 occasionally emit broad branches, more slender and longer in the ♂ than in the ♀; frequently too, they are only slightly compressed and subserrate, in this case the second joint is very distinct and one-half as long as the third. The sexual characters are simple; the ventral segments are seven in the ♀, the seventh being large and slightly nicked at the tip; they are eight in the ♂, the seventh being broadly and strongly emarginate, and the eighth elongate-oval, moderate in size and prominent. There are slight differences in the form of the two last segments of ♂ in our species, but as they are readily recognized by other characters I have not deemed it prudent to encumber the tables with minutiæ of such small import which would probably tend to confuse the student.

The genera represented in our fauna may be divided into three natural groups: the first is typical and peculiar, the second tends to the Lampyridæ (gen.), and the third to the Telephoridæ.

Prothoracic spiracle not prominent. ....2.
Prothoracic spiracle with tubular chitinous peritreme, very prominent in the usual position of the epimeron, behind and at the outer extremity of the front coxæ. (except in *Cænia*)..LYCI.
2.—Elytra costate, cancellate or reticulate...EROTES.
    Elytra substriate, not costate or cancellate.................. ............LYGISTOPTERI.

Group 1.—*Lyci.*
Front prolonged, beak more or less distinct, mouth anterior...................... ....2.
Front gibbous between the antennæ, mouth deflexed, inferior, beak wanting.......4.
2.—Beak long. ....3.
    Beak short..**RHYNCHEROS** n. g.
3. - Antennæ with third joint as long as fourth and fifth........ ....**LYCUS.**
    Antennæ with third joint scarcely longer than fourth..............**LYCOSTOMUS.**
4.—Antennæ much compressed...**CALOPTERON.**
    Antennæ pectinate; spiracle prominent.....................................**CELETES.**
    Antennæ pectinate; spiracle not prominent........... ....**CÆNIA.**

LYCUS Fabr.

Beak long, maxillary palpi with last joint longer than wide, rounded on inner side; antennæ compressed, serrate, second joint short, third as long as the two following. Prothorax carinate near the apex, then channeled, forming a narrow areolet, sides broadly reflexed, without ridges. Elytra with four fine costæ, interspaces transversely rugose, sides very broadly dilated, especially in ♂.

Scarlet-red, apical one-fourth of elytra, head, antennæ, tarsi and tibiæ, (except on inner edge), black; ♂ seventh ventral deeply and broadly emarginate, eighth spathiform, flattened at base and faintly bisulcate; tibiæ feebly curved, trochanters triangular, not acute. Length 8.5–13 mm. L. Cala.: Ariz..........**cruentus** Lec.

The specimens from Arizona are much more broadly dilated on the sides of the elytra than those from Lower California, but are probably not specifically distinct.

LYCOSTOMUS Motsch.

Characters as in *Lycus*, except that the last joint of the maxillary palpi is truncate at tip; prothorax less carinate in front, and less channeled behind; elytra less dilated on the sides, rather finely reticulate between the costæ; third joint of antennæ scarcely longer than fourth. None of these differences seem to me of generic value.

Black, prothorax at apex and sides, and sides of elytra as far as the middle fulvous; prothorax with the sides flattened and broadly reflexed, apex oblique each side, obtusely angulated at the middle; finely carinate in front, feebly channeled behind. Elytra with suture, margin and four costæ elevated, the third abbreviated at each end, feeble and sometimes obsolete, interspaces finely reticulate with a slight tendency here and there to form double rows: sides slightly and suddenly dilated; trochanters with lower angle sharp; ♂ seventh ventral deeply semicircularly emarginate, eighth smooth, prolonged, narrow, rounded at tip; last dorsal moderately prolonged; middle and hind tibiæ strongly curved. Length 8—10 mm. Pa.; Ga.; Tex..........................:....................**lateralis** Mels.

a.—Elytra fulvous from base for two-thirds the length, suture black; Fla.

Black, sides of prothorax, and of fifth and sixth ventral segments, elytra and seventh and eighth ventral segments, pale red; prothorax less carinate in front, more broadly channeled behind; elytra similarly but more strongly sculptured with the reticulations in regular rows: scutel black, truncate behind; middle and hind tibiæ less curved; ♀. Length 13 mm. Col.; Dr. Horn, one specimen.

fulvellus n. sp.

The third joint of the antennæ is comparatively longer, and the following joints shorter than in *L. lateralis*.

RHYNCHEROS n. g.

Lycus sanguinipennis Say, differs so much from all the other Eros-like forms in having a distinct beak and tubular prothoracic spiracles, that I have been compelled to separate it as a distinct genus. The head is prolonged into a broad beak, as long as wide and narrowed in front;

the last joint of the palpi is triangular, not longer than wide; the eyes
are moderate and convex in both sexes. Antennæ one-half as long
as the body, widely compressed, second joint short but distinct, third
elongate triangular, longer than fourth; 4—10 subtriangular, outer side
sinuate and rounded, distal side not oblique, angle acute. Prothorax
with sides very widely reflexed, not thickened, apex slightly prominent
at the middle and feebly nicked; disc feebly carinate near the apex, then
with a deep channel extending to the base. Scutel truncate behind.
Elytra suddenly but not widely dilated on the sides which are rounded;
discoidal costæ four, which are very feeble, except the fourth is prominent
and acute at the humeri; interspaces irregularly reticulate; suture and
margin scarcely elevated.

It is a singular species leading from *Lycus* to *Plateros*.

Black, sides of prothorax and the whole of the elytra bright scarlet; prothorax
slightly carinate at tip, rather strongly channeled behind, sides broadly reflexed,
front angles rounded, hind angles acute; scutel black; ♀ with sides of elytra
more suddenly and more broadly dilated; seventh ventral deeply rather squarely
emarginate, the side lobes of the emargination passing under the transverse
anterior edge; tibiæ very slightly curved, angle of trochanters rounded. Length
10 mm. Col...**sanguinipennis** Say.

CALOPTERON Newm.

This genus seems to be natural, if defined by the following characters,
though if slight differences in the reticulation of the elytra are exaggerated
in importance it can doubtless be divided into several genera, which would
be widely separated by that character.

Beak wanting, front short, gibbous, mouth inflexed; maxillary palpi
long, dilated, last joint transverse, distal side oblique. Antennæ long,
strongly compressed, joints broad, the outer ones frequently broader than
the others, second joint very short, third not as long as the fourth.
Prothorax strongly carinate for the whole length, sides reflexed; scutel
acute, small. Elytra wider behind, gradually, but sometimes very strongly
dilated, costate, and coarsely reticulate.

Elytra with four discoidal costæ..2.
Elytra with three discoidal costæ..3.
2.—Costæ equally strong..3.
　　Second and fourth costæ very feeble..4.
3.—Prothorax small, not wider than long, sides yellow; elytra sinuate on the
　　sides, six times wider behind than at base, reticulations quadrate, single
　　at base, becoming double behind: yellow, with a transverse band at the
　　anterior one-third, and the apical one-fourth blue-black; legs at base
　　tinged with fulvous: ♀ seventh ventral deeply emarginate, eighth parallel,
　　narrow, elongated, rounded at tip. Length 11.5—15 mm. Oregon.
　　　　　　　　　　　　　　　　　　　　　　　　　　　　megalopteron Lec.

Prothorax small, not longer than wide, black, sides usually yellow, elytra not sinuate on the sides, about four times wider behind than at the base, reticulations wider than long, irregularly divided in places; fulvous, apical one-third black; frequently with a more or less perfect broad black band in front of the middle; ♂ seventh ventral emarginate, eighth parallel, rounded at tip, side valves usually visible, rounded at tip.   Length 11—16 mm. Atlantic region ; Cal..**reticulatum** Fabr.

   a.—Transverse black band of elytra not extending to the sides.   *D. dorsalis* Newm.; *duplicatum* Hald.

   β.—Transverse black band wanting, *terminale* Say.

4.—Prothorax wider than long, sides usually rarely entirely black fulvous, more broadly reflexed; elytra not sinuate on the sides, about three times wider behind than at base, first and third costae finer and less elevated than the second and fourth, reticulations wider than long, irregularly divided in a few places; fulvous, apical one-third black; also with a broad black band in front of the middle extending along the suture to the base; ♂ seventh ventral emarginate, eighth elongate, narrowed towards the tip.   Length 11.5—19 mm.   Atlantic region..................................**typicum** Newm.

   a.—Band of elytra not extending along the suture, sometimes not attaining the sides; *affine* Lec.

   β.—Band of elytra wanting: *divisum* Newm.; *apicale* Lec.

Prothorax smaller and more triangular, otherwise similar to *typicum*, except that the first and third costae of the elytra are very feeble, and the reticulations are not transverse but mostly quadrate.   Length 8.5—11 mm.   Ariz., one ♀ ; Mr. Bolter...**retiferum** n. sp.

   a.—Elytral band very narrow, scarcely attaining the sides; Col., one ♂ : seventh ventral deeply emarginate, eighth elongate, narrowed towards the tip.

5.—Narrower than the other species, proportioned like *Celetes basalis*, black, prothorax and elytra fulvous ; the former a little wider than long, sides sinuate, apex bisinuate and angulated at the middle, tip of the angle rounded ; front angles prominent, rounded, hind angles acute, prolonged, carina of disc strong, dusky ; sides concave, margin reflexed ; scutel fulvous, impressed, nicked behind.   Elytra gradually slightly wider, one-third wider behind than at base ; suture, margin, and three discoidal costae strongly elevated, reticulation somewhat transverse ; antennae strongly serrate, joints 3—10 nearly equal in length, broadly triangular, anterior side curved, distal side oblique, angle acute ; last joint of maxillary palpi longer than wide, parallel on the sides, rounded at tip.   Length 9 mm.   Ariz., one ♀ ; Mr. Bolter.

tricarinatum n. sp.

This species by the form of the palpi, antennae, and number of elytral costae, seems to indicate a distinct genus, to which a name has probably been already attached, though I have failed to identify it in any of the works within my reach.

Calopteron retiferum.—Black, beneath mouth and joints of legs and base of antennae tinged with testaceous.   Antennae two-thirds as long as the body, very broadly compressed, second joint very short, inconspicuous, third not as long as the fourth, outer ones gradually a little narrower.   Palpi broadly dilated, last joint trapezoidal, broader than long. Prothorax small, strongly carinate, sides strongly reflexed, obliquely converging in front, hind angles long, divergent, disc dusky. Elytra with the humeri and a narrow transverse band about the middle fulvous; sides gradually and moderately dilated, regularly rounded behind; surface hairy, suture, margin and two discoidal costae strongly elevated; first and second interspaces with double series of large cells which are not very transverse, as in *reticulatum*, but quadrate. Length 6.7 mm.

Arizona, one ♀, kindly given me by Prof. C. V. Riley. The reticulation of the elytra is almost as in *Cænia dimidiata*, but the form of body, antennæ, palpi and arrangement of color are as in *Calopteron typicum*.

Calopteron tricarinatum.—Black, above fulvous: eyes rather large, convex, palpi with the last joint trapezoidal, not longer than wide. Antennæ very broad, two-thirds as long as the body, second joint very small, third triangular, longer than fourth, 4—10 triangular, not longer than wide, outer side curved, distal side oblique, angle rather acute, eleventh longer, oval, subsinuate near the tip. Prothorax broader than long, narrowed in front, apex subangulate, sides sinuate, broadly reflexed, hind angles divergent, acute, disc very strongly carinate. Scutel triangular, slightly nicked behind. Elytra elongate, subparallel, but slightly wider behind, suture, margin and three discoidal costae strongly elevated, interspaces with large quadrate reticulations which are not more than twice as wide as long. Beneath tinged with testaceous. Length 7 mm.

Arizona, one ♀, for which I am also indebted to Prof. C. V. Riley. The form of the last joint of the palpi seems to require the reference of this species to Calopteron, though the reticulation of the elytra and the form of antennæ are quite different. It seems to belong to the Section A, ii, of Biologia Centro-Americana, (Lycidae. p 13), in which case the ♂ antennæ would be pectinate.

CÆNIA Newm.

Although in this genus the prothoracic spiracle is not tubular and prominent, yet in all other respects it resembles so closely the preceding genera, especially *Calopteron*, that it cannot be naturally separated from them. The front is strongly gibbous, prolonged into a very short triangular beak; maxillary palpi dilated, last joint elongate, cultriform, the outer margin sinuate, the inner one rounded into the tip, which is obtuse. Antennæ very broadly compressed, first joint broad, triangular, second very short, third one-half as long as fourth, 4—10 broad, in ♂ each with a long basal process, in ♀ with a shorter and broader medial process gradually occupying the whole length of the joint, eleventh joint elongate, rounded at tip. Prothorax strongly carinate, sides broadly reflexed, sinuate, front angles rounded, hind angles acute, prolonged, apex bisinuate, prominent and rounded at the middle. Scutel triangular, slightly nicked behind. Elytra with four discoidal costae, first and third less elevated, interspaces with double rows of coarse quadrate reticulations.

Black, sides of prothorax and anterior half of elytra fulvous, with the exception of a scutellar black spot; sides broadly dilated and rounded, about three times as wide behind as at base: legs tinged with yellow at base, trochanters long, narrow; ♂ seventh ventral feebly emarginate, eighth elongate, rounded at tip. Length 10 mm. Atlantic region..**dimidiata** Fabr.

a.—Prothorax black.

Black, sides and apex of prothorax, and sides of elytra to the middle fulvous; elytra only one-half wider behind than at base; reticulations longer than wide, trochanters shorter and more triangular; ♀ antennæ with the joints broader, triangular with rounded side and acute angle. Length 10 mm. Colorado; Prof. F. H. Snow...**amplicornis** n. sp.

Cænia amplicornis.—Black, prothorax in great part, and sides of elytra from base to middle dull fulvous. Head channeled, eyes moderate in size, convex, palpi broad with last joint elongated, oval, subacute at tip. Antennæ one-half as long as the body, very broadly compressed, second joint very short, hardly visible, third shorter than fourth, triangular, 4—10 wider, not as long as wide, outer side convexly curved, distal side oblique, angle subacute, last joint longer, oval. Prothorax wider than long, not narrowed in front, apex sinuate, rounded at the middle, sides very oblique near the front angles, then abruptly rounded and parallel, hind angle small, acute, strongly divergent: disc concave, strongly carinate, fulvous, with a large posterior blackish spot. Scutel triangular, emarginate behind. Elytra elongate, gradually but slightly broader behind, suture, margin and four discoidal costæ elevated, first, second and fourth extending nearly to the tip and uniting as usual, third elevated for only about one-fourth the length, then finer and less elevated, not different from the lines of reticulation: interspaces each with two rows of reticulations, nearly all of which are longer than wide; sides broadly fulvous from base to the middle. Length 10 mm.

Colorado: one ♀. Prof. F. H. Snow. Resembles in form and color *Celetes basalis* and *Eros humeralis*, but very different by the antennæ which are like those of *Calopteron tricarinatum*, but are still wider.

CELETES Newm.

Front gibbous, beak none, mouth inflexed, maxillary palpi with the last joint acute, a little longer than wide, and longer than third joint. Antennæ long, first joint triangular, second very short, third wider and shorter than fourth, 4—10 with a long basal process (♂); or shorter broadly triangular with acute angle (♀). Scutel truncate and nicked behind. Prothorax strongly carinate, sides reflexed. Elytra gradually becoming twice as wide behind as at base; suture, margin and four discoidal costæ acutely elevated, interspaces with single rows of coarse reticulations, which are quadrate and not transverse. This genus osculates with the next group.

The prothorax is very variable in form in this species.

Black, sides of prothorax and humeral line of elytra fulvous, base of thighs yellowish; ♂ seventh ventral emarginate, eighth elongate, narrow, rounded at tip. Length 6—8.5 mm. Atlantic region.....................................**basalis** Lec.

a.—The prothorax varies greatly in size and form, being usually larger in ♀ than ♂; the elytra sometimes much less dilated behind. These differences account for the names by which in my inexperience I distinguished two nominal species.

Group 2.—*Erotes.*

In this group the front is short, gibbous, sometimes transversely margined, the beak is wanting and the mouth deflexed; the last joint of the maxillary palpi is longer than the preceding, acute at tip.

The antennae are moderately compressed, with the second joint usually at least one-half as long as the third, which is not longer than the fourth. Prothorax carinate, divided into cells or feebly channeled; spiracle not tubular, depressed. Elytra reticulate, costate and cancellate, or with ribs scarcely elevated and interstices with single small quadrate depressions, never widely dilated behind. Front coxae rather narrowly separated.

Prothorax strongly carinate, sides divided by an oblique ridge from the hind angles..**LOPHEROS** n. g.
Prothorax many celled, sides divided by a strong transverse ridge..............**EROS**.
Prothorax not carinate, feebly channeled behind, sides not divided by transverse ridge..**PLATEROS**.

LOPHEROS n. g.

Lycus fraternus differs so remarkably from the other Eros-like forms in our fauna, that I have felt disposed to separate it as a distinct genus, not however, without perceiving that a more careful study of foreign forms may lead to the suppression of this with *Plateros*, and some other dismemberments suggested by Mr. Waterhouse into *Eros*.

The eyes are small and lateral, widely separated in both sexes, the head transversely impressed between the eyes, front channeled, convex. Antennae moderately serrate, first joint triangular, equal to the third, second triangular, wider than long, one-third the length of the third, 4—10 very gradually longer and narrower, eleventh one-third longer than tenth. Prothorax wider than long, narrowed in front, strongly carinate nearly to the base, disc deeply concave, sides strongly reflexed, oblique, sinuate, hind angles prolonged outward, with an oblique carinate, reaching neither the angle nor the median ridge. Scutel elongate, nearly parallel, emarginate behind. Elytra gradually and slightly widened behind, with suture, margin and four discoidal strongly elevated costae, interspaces goffred or waffled, with double rows of quadrate cells. Trochanters triangular, not elongate. Seventh ventral ♂ deeply emarginate, eighth elongate, narrower and pointed at tip.

Black, prothorax with a large transverse fulvous spot behind the middle. Length 9—11 mm. New England and Northern New York............**fraternus** Randall.

EROS Newm.

Prothorax with five well-defined cells, the medial one rhombic, not carinate......;2.

Prothorax with six cells, sometimes ill-defined, the middle anterior one more or less carinate...6.

2.—Upper surface scarlet...3.

Upper surface in great part black, humeral spot and sometimes the sides of prothorax fulvous; antennæ with elongate, slender joints, second and third united, scarcely as long as the fourth, trochanters triangular. Length 5—8 mm. Maine: Lake Superior............................**thoracicus** Rand.

3.—Antennæ slender, third joint shorter than fourth; legs red............................4.

Antennæ stouter, third joint equal to fourth...5.

4.—Red, antennæ black, first joint red: ventral segments, sides of metathorax and tarsi dark; trochanters of hind legs very long, acute at the angle: middle trochanters also spinose but shorter; ♂ antennæ more than one-half as long as the body, second and third joints united, not longer than fourth; ♀ antennæ shorter, trochanters less acutely spinose. Length 13.5-- 16 mm. Alaska; Vancouver..**hamatus** Mann.

Black beneath, red above, first joint of antennæ and legs red, tarsi dusky; trochanters short, triangular, not acute; ♂ antennæ one-half as long as the body, second and third joints united equal to fourth; ♀ antennæ shorter, third joint nearly equal to fourth. Length 8.5—11 mm. Alaska; Oregon. **simplicipes** Mann.

5.—Very similar to *simplicipes* but the antennæ are stouter, and distinctly serrate upper surface, first joint of antennæ and legs red, tarsi dusky; trochanters triangular. Length 8.5—13 mm. Vanc.; Or.: Cala.........**lætus** Motsch.

Black, upper surface scarlet; trochanters triangular, antennæ less than one-half as long as the body: legs black. Length 6—10.5 mm. L. Sup.; Ga.; Can.; Or..**coccineus** Say.

Colored and formed like *hamatus*, much smaller, trochanters long but not spinose; antennæ with first and second joints red: in ♂ more than one-half as long as the body, slightly serrate, second and third joints united equal to the fourth; in ♀ shorter and stouter, third joint comparatively larger. Length 6 mm. Georgia..**mundus** Say.

6.—Head not strongly margined before the antennæ..7.

Head strongly margined in front; EROTIDES Waterhouse.

Black, prothorax red, sometimes with black disc, six-celled, anterior middle cell quadrate, carinate, posterior middle cell narrow; antennæ elongate, slender, third joint but little shorter than fourth, second less than one-half as long; trochanters long; ♂ antennæ longer, outer joints narrower, front more strongly margined, trochanters longer, tibiæ less compressed than usual and slightly bent; ♀ trochanters shorter, more triangular, tibiæ not bent. Length 5—7 mm. Southern States......................**sculptilis** Say.

7.—Anterior middle cell of prothorax with the sides indistinct, strongly carinate at the middle, posterior middle cell narrow, like a channel; transverse carinæ between the anterior and posterior rows of cells strong, sinuate;* antennæ as in *sculptilis* but second joint a little larger: trochanters triangular and tibiæ straight in both sexes; ♀ antennæ shorter and stouter. Length 8—10 mm. Atlantic slope...............................**humeralis** Fab.

---

* The posterior lateral cells are imperfectly divided by a short transverse ridge proceeding from the median posterior cell. This species (*humeralis*) is a central

a.—Prothorax fulvous, with a brownish spot, anterior one-half or two-thirds of elytra fulvous. Mo.; Ks.; Tex.

β.—Prothorax fulvous, sometimes with disc dark, elytra with more or less extensive humeral spot; (type form).

γ.—Elytra black, sometimes with a very small humeral spot; prothorax black, with margins narrowly fulvous, *incestus* Lec. L. Sup.; Pa.; Mass.

Black, sides of prothorax fulvous; walls of anterior series of prothoracic cells obliterated, only the medial carina remaining: posterior row of cells as in the preceding; viz., a narrow deep medial one, (which is very finely carinate at base), and two large lateral ones defined by the usual transverse ridge; the lateral cell is divided a transverse obtuse prominence into a deep impression, and a strongly marked subbasal groove. Scutel and elytra as usual, the latter 4-costate the interspaces with double rows of quadrate cells: trochanters large triangular, tibiæ straight; antennæ of ♂ long, slender, scarcely serrate, third joint less than one-half as long as fourth; of ♀ shorter, stouter, subserrate, third joint one-half as long as fourth. Length 5—7.5 mm. N. J.; Ga.....................**trilineatus** Mels.

a.—First discoidal costa of elytra indistinct; eyes of ♂ larger than in type. Ill.; Va.; Fla.

Black, prothorax fulvous, walls of anterior middle cell very indistinct, carina acute, strongly marked, extending from apex to base, the posterior middle cell having disappeared, transverse ridge strong, extending from margin to dorsal carina, posterior lateral cells with a short transverse convexity connected with the dorsal carina. Elytra 4-costate, interspaces with double rows of quadrate cells; trochanters triangular, tibiæ straight; antennæ of ♂ slightly serrate, third joint broad, triangular, two-thirds as long as the fourth; of ♀ rather stouter, but not otherwise specially different. Length 5.5—7.5 mm. N. Y.; Me.; L. Sup ....**crenatus** Germ.

PLATEROS Bourgeois, (4 Waterh.).

In this genus the prothorax is without cells, sometimes slightly carinate at the apex, always channeled or impressed behind the middle; the sides are strongly reflexed, but without the transverse ridge seen in the genuine Eros. The scutel is flat, truncate behind. Elytra with rows of quadrate cells separated by nine narrow and usually equal slightly elevated lines; sometimes the alternate lines are a little stronger, so that they become feebly 4-costate. The species of this genus are found on both continents, and are still very indistinctly defined.

one, with which by modifications in different directions the other forms can be readily harmonized: thus by completing the side walls of the anterior median cell you have *sculptilis*, by obliterating the walls of the anterior median cell and retaining the carina you have *trilineatus;* by making the middle posterior cell vanish, but retaining a carina to represent its walls, you have *crenatus;* finally by obliterating the cell walls of the disc, retaining only the basal part of the middle posterior cell, with the imperfect transverse elevated line connected with it, you pass over to the genus *Plateros.* We have here evidently a complex in which not only supposed generic characters are untenable, but the species are also somewhat plastic and difficult to define.

Among the species cited by Mr. Bourgeois under this genus (Comptes-rendus Soc. Ent. Belg. 1879, xix), is *Lycus sanguinipennis* Say. What is signified by that name is not Say's species, which will be found above under *Rhyncheros*, but a beautiful scarlet species of the present genus found in Mexico. It was collected by Mr. Sallé, to whom I am indebted for a specimen, and has been described (Dec. 1880), in Biologia Cent. Am. Lycidae, p. 21, tab. 2, f. 16, as *P. lateritius*; the reference to Bourgeois' mention of this insect is omitted.

The species in this genus are almost undistinguishable. I have found no characters for separating them except the form of the antennae, especially in the ♂.

Antennae broad, very strongly compressed, third joint as wide as long, not as large as the fourth; 4—10 gradually longer and narrower, the lower ones as wide as long, the ninth about twice as long as wide, anterior angle somewhat acute,...2.

Antennae less broad, more distinctly serrate, the joints being narrower at base and triangular rather than trapezoidal, second joint more rounded, third triangular, as wide as the fourth but not as long, 4—10 gradually narrower, but scarcely increasing in length, fifth about twice as long as wide.........3.

2.—Black, prothorax fulvous, with a large discoidal blackish spot very feebly carinate at tip, dorsal cellule wide, posterior or basal outline well defined, lateral outlines almost obliterated; elytra with the alternate interstitial lines distinctly elevated, the others rather irregular and indistinct with coarser cells than in *modestus*; ♂ seventh dorsal more deeply and widely emarginate than in that species, eighth larger and wider than usual. Length 5—7.5 mm. Va.; Ga.; Fla..**timidus** Lec.
  α.—Prothorax black with the sides fulvous; Fla.
  β.—Prothorax black with very narrow fulvous side margin; Fla.

3.—Black, prothorax with sides and narrow apical and basal margin fulvous, not carinate at apex, basal cellule short, basal and lateral margin elevated; elytra with alternate interstitial lines more elevated, intermediate ones very indistinct; antennae of ♂ with joints triangular, third one-half as long as fourth, but not wider; fifth twice as long as wide, outer ones gradually narrower, the angle not acute, and the distal sides of the joints are therefore not oblique; of ♀ similar to those of ♂ but somewhat broader; seventh ventral ♂ broadly emarginate, eighth elongate, of usual form. Length 5.5—7.5 mm. L. Sup.; Pa...................................**modestus** Say.

Black, prothorax with sides and frequently apical and basal margin, also the humeri fulvous; apex not carinate, basal cellule a narrow channel extending nearly to the middle; elytra with interstitial lines equal, or nearly so; antennae rather strongly serrate as above described, except that the angle is distinctly acute and the distal edge oblique. Length 5—8 mm. L. Sup.; Pa.; Fla. Varies greatly both in size and form, as does also the preceding species, so that the synonyms are quite numerous...**canaliculatus** Say.
  α.—As above, alternate interspaces more elevated.
  β.—Humeri and anterior part of suture fulvous.
  γ.—Entirely black.

Very similar to *canaliculatus* but narrower, prothorax fulvous with a large black spot, sides more strongly reflexed, apex not carinate, base emarginate at the middle, dorsal canal extending from base to the middle: elytra with well marked equal lines and strongly cancellate interspaces; antennæ of ♂ long, joints as in *canaliculatus*, fourth fully twice as long as third; fifth twice as long as wide, outer ones narrower, with angle acute and distal side oblique; front twice as wide as the diameter of the eyes; seventh ventral deeply emarginate, eighth elongated; antennæ of ♀ shorter, less serrate; seventh joint twice as long as wide, dorsal channel of prothorax deeper. Length 5—8 mm. Pa.; Ga.; Fla..............................**sollicitus** Lec.

Also narrower than *canaliculatus*, prothorax black, sides fulvous, apex not carinate, base straight, cellule elongate, forming a dorsal channel extending to the middle in ♂, broader and shorter in ♀; elytra with well marked equal lines and more finely cancellate interspaces; antennæ of ♂ long, distinctly serrate, third joint triangular, as wide as long, fourth longer, not wider, fifth twice as long as wide, outer ones narrower, distal side oblique and angle acute, eyes large; antennæ of ♀ broader, less serrate, eighth joint twice as long as wide; eyes smaller; seventh ventral of ♂ emarginate, eighth elongate, narrowed and subacute at tip. Length 5—7 mm. N. J.; Ga.; Fla..**lictor** Newm.

Very similar to the preceding, but differs by the antennæ in both sexes shorter and less strongly serrate. Length 4—5.5 mm. N. Y.; Pa.; Ga.

floralis Mels.

Group 3.—*Lygistopteri*.

The insects of this group, of which two genera are represented in our fauna are easily distinguished by the pubescent velvety surface, and the feebly striate, not reticulated elytra. The head is prolonged into a long or short broad beak, which latter form is rather a muzzle, like that of many *Podabri;* the eyes are moderate and the front broad; the antennæ are rather widely separated, subserrate, with the joints thicker and less compressed than in the other two groups; the second joint is one-half as long as third, which is shorter than fourth. Maxillary palpi with last joint subtriangular, apical side oblique. Prothorax channeled, margins usually thickened, reflexed, with an oblique ridge running forwards towards the median groove; the thickened side of the prothorax is usually foveate at the middle of its length, thus recalling *Polemius* of the Telephoridæ, as the form of the muzzle does *Podabrus*.

Beak long, narrowed at tip. Prothoracic channel forming a rhombic cell, the sides of which connect with the oblique ridge, sides not thickened. Maxillary palpi with distal side of last joint curved...................................**LYGISTOPTERUS**.
Beak short, broad. Prothorax with thickened sides, oblique ridges short. Maxillary palpi with distal side of last joint oblique...................................**CALOCHROMUS**.

LYGISTOPTERUS Muls.

But one species is known to me in our fauna.

Black, velvety pubescent, with the elytra scarlet. Length 11—12.5 mm. Colorado.

rubripennis Lec.

28

J. L. LECONTE. M. D.

CALOCHROMUS Guer.

Lateral margin of prothorax impressed at the middle............2.
Lateral margin of prothorax not impressed; black, prothorax and elytra scarlet, the former with a transverse posterior dusky spot, tibiæ straight. Length 9 mm. Col., one ♀; Dr. Horn............**fervens** n. sp.
2.—Prothorax finely channeled. ....3.
Prothorax strongly channeled, black, sides of prothorax fulvous; middle and hind tibiæ curved. Length 6—9.5 mm. Atl. region.....**perfacetus** Say.
a.—Prothorax entirely fulvous; Texas. ♂ ♀.
3.—Blue-black, prothorax scarlet; middle and hind tibiæ curved. Length 7—9.5 mm. Col.; Or............**ruficollis** Lec.
Black, prothorax and anterior half of elytra scarlet, scutel black; tibiæ straight. Length 8 mm. Cala.; Nev............**dimidiatus** Lec.

C. fervens.—Black, velvety with extremely fine short pubescence. Head with a broad shallow slightly channeled impression between the eyes which are small and convex: muzzle extremely short, beak none; antennæ one-half as long as the body, second joint about one-half as long as the third, which is equal to the fourth: joints moderately compressed, about twice as long as wide, distal side slightly oblique. Palpi short with last joint triangular. Prothorax quadrate, one-half wider than long, front angles rounded: sides thickened and reflexed, with a strong ridge running from the middle of the sides obliquely and slightly forwards on to the disc which is only feebly channeled near the base: the posterior excavation between the strong basal margin and the ridges is dusky. Scutel black, truncate behind. Elytra scarlet, closely but indistinctly striate with rows of shallow punctures, not reticulated; elongate, parallel, narrowly margined, but little wider than the prothorax. Tibiæ not curved. Length 9 mm.

Colorado, one ♀: Dr. Horn. Related to *perfacetus* but differs by the color, by the thickened side margin of the prothorax not impressed at the side, by the disc being very slightly channeled, and finally by the head being quite without beak. Species apparently congeneric with the four here tabulated are cited in Biol. Centr. Amer. as belonging to *Lygistopterus,*

Sub-family II.—LAMPYRIDÆ.

The species of this sub-family are easily separated from the Lycidæ by the middle coxæ being contiguous, and the epipleuræ wide at the base of the elytra, even when the latter as in some ♀ ♀ are very short.

From the Telephoridæ they are known by the metathoracic episterna being sinuate on the inner margin, a character first observed by Duval, and which seems to me to have much value in apportioning the more difficult forms to their respective groups.

The genera examined seem to indicate two tribes: the first is numerous on both continents, especially in the tropical regions: the second is perhaps exclusively American, unless it can be united with Drilini.
Head more or less covered, antennæ approximate or moderately distant; metathoracic epimera long............LAMPYRINI.
Head exposed, antennæ distant; metathoracic epimera wide............PHENGODINI.

Tribe 1.—LAMPYRINI.

The most characteristic structure in these insects is the light-giving apparatus which is contained in the posterior abdominal segments of most of the species, though it is quite absent in some genera.

The position and form of the organs differ according to genus and in a less degree according to species.

In most of the genera the sexes are similar in appearance, but in the Lampyres group the ♀ are larger than ♂ and larviform, with short elytra and no wings. In these genera the eyes of the ♂ have their maximum, and those of the ♀ the minimum development. In the other groups the eyes of the ♂ though larger than those of ♀, are not remarkable or disproportionate in size. The head is deeply immersed in the prothorax which is foliate at the sides and apex, so as to protect the head.

The antennae are approximate or moderately separated, and vary in form according to group and genus. Our genera seem to indicate the following groups:

Antennae with second joint small, usually transverse, head completely covered by prothorax.
    Antennae pectinate, rather distant, last joint simple..........................*Mathetei.*
    Antennae not pectinate, (in our genera), approximate, last joint elongate, simple..*Photini.*
    Antennae with last joint appendiculate, having a small acicular appendage.
                                   Lampyres.
Antennae with second joint not transverse: head exserted, narrowed behind the eyes...*Luciolæ.*

Group 1.— *Mathetei.*

In this group the front is wide, the antennae moderately separated at the base, eleven-jointed, pectinate or bipectinate, with the last joint elongate, sinuate and pointed at tip. The eyes are not very large, lateral, convex, widely separated above and beneath.

The prothorax is less prolonged over the head than in the next two groups; the elytra are similar in both sexes and the inflexed epipleuræ are wide near the base, the extreme margin being reflexed and elevated as far as the length of the metasternum; this fold is parallel with the side margin in *Matheteus*, but runs obliquely towards the latter in *Polyclasis*.

Margins expanded, flattened; antennae pectinate......................**MATHETEUS.**
Margins not flattened; antennae bipectinate......................... ....**POLYCLASIS.**

MATHETEUS Lec.

Antennae with second joint small, third triangular, oblique, anterior side short; joints 4—10 with a long flat process about the middle; eleventh elongate-oval, acute, with a cusp on the anterior side near the tip.

Black, upper surface rose-colored; prothorax with two black spots; sixth ventral segment with a small acute emargination, seventh rounded at tip.   Length 11.5 mm.
♂. Mariposa, Cala...**Theveneti** Lec.

POLYCLASIS Newm. (emend.)

Antennæ bipectinate, (♂ strongly, ♀ less so), from third to tenth joint; second joint small, third not shorter than fourth ; pectinations at the base of the joints in ♂ ; at the middle of the sides in ♀, and becoming shorter on the outer joints which are nearly simple; eleventh joint sinuate near the tip.

Mr. Gorham retains this genus as distinct from *Calyptocephalus*, but I do not know upon what characters the difference is established.

Elongate-oval, black, scabrous punctured, prothorax with sides and apex fulvous, dorsal channel distinct ; ♂ seventh and eighth ventral segments testaceous, seventh with a small triangular incision, eighth narrow, parallel ; ♀ sixth and seventh testaceous, the latter triangular, rounded behind.   Length 10 mm.   Ohio.
bifaria Say.

Group 2.—*Photini*.

In this group the antennæ are more or less compressed, sometimes serrate ; the last joint is elongate and rounded at tip, without appendages or sinuation ; the second joint is short, sometimes very short and transverse (*Lucidota*).   The sexes are similar in appearance except in one species of *Photinus*, where the elytra of the ♀ are short and the wings wanting.   The eyes are larger in ♂ than ♀, but are separated by a wide space both above and beneath in all the species.   In the ♂ the last ventral segment is small and narrow, covered by the scutate last dorsal, which varies in form according to genus and species.   The light organs, when present, are more developed in ♂ than ♀, which is the reverse of what obtains in the group Lampyres.   The head is always covered by the hood-like prothorax.   The epipleuræ of the elytra are wide at the base ; the inferior (or distal) margin is reflexed, and converges more or less to the lateral margin of the elytra.   The elytra vary in color ; in the species without well-developed light organs they are black, with the single exception of *Pyropyga indicta*, where they are brown margined with testaceous, as in the brilliantly luminous species.

It will therefore be especially necessary for the inexperienced student to ascertain in this group, to what genus his specimen should be referred, before he attempts its specific determination.

There are in many families of Coleoptera strong resemblances between species of different genera, but I know of none (with the exception of certain Rhynchophora), so deceptive as those which our own limited fauna presents to us in this group of Lampyridæ.

Eyes small; light organs feeble; ventral segments without stigma-like pores......2.
Eyes large, but larger in ♂ than ♀; light organs well developed; ♂ with strongly marked stigma-like ventral pores,...................... ....5.
2.—Antennæ with second joint one-half as long as third or nearly so............ 3.
Antennæ very much compressed, not serrate, second joint very short, transverse..**LUCIDOTA.**
3.—Antennæ not serrate, narrow, compressed..4.
Antennæ strongly serrate (♂ ♀), prothorax subcarinate, dorsal abdominal segments strongly lobed, ♂ last dorsal broadly emarginate.....**TENASPIS** n. g.
4. – Last dorsal segment ♂ rounded.................. ....**ELLYCHNIA.**
Last dorsal segment ♂ bisinuate and truncate.......................**PYROPYGA.**
5.—Prothorax subcarinate; ♀ with lateral light organs.........**PYRACTOMENA.**
Prothorax not carinate, frequently channeled ; ♀ with medial light organs.
PHOTINUS.

LUCIDOTA Lap. *Lychnuris* Motsch.

This genus is easily known by the very broadly compressed antennæ, which are not serrate, gradually narrowed externally, and with the second joint very short and transverse. The light organs are very feebly developed, and indicated by yellow spots on the last ventral (♀), or last two ventrals (♂). The dorsal segments are acutely lobed at the sides in both sexes, with the lobes directed backwards. In the ♂ the last dorsal is truncato-emarginate and the seventh ventral is biemarginate, the middle lobe being quite distinct.

To this genus belongs the Mexican *L. thoracica* (Oliv.), in which the prothorax is yellow, the scutel testaceous, and the ventral segments entirely black. .

These insects are diurnal and are frequently seen flying in shady places; when seized they exude from the joints of the legs and the sides of the body a milky fluid with a disagreeable odor.

Large, black, sides and apical margin of prothorax fulvous; ♂ ♀. Length 7—11 mm. N. Y.; Ga.; Ill...**atra** Fabr.
a.—Prothorax black, with very narrow yellow margin ; *tarda* Lec.
Small, narrow, prothorax pale, dorsal spot and basal margin black, disc with two rosy spots; ♂ last four ventral segments gradually testaceous. Length 6 mm. Middle and Southern States.............................**punctata** Lec.
a.—Hind angles of prothorax blackish.

ELLYCHNIA Lec.

The antennæ are narrow, usually not serrate, but always strongly compressed, with the second joint but little wider than long, and about one-half as long as the third, which is not longer than the fourth. The dorsal segments are not acutely lobed at the sides, and except the penultimate are not produced backwards. The last dorsal is truncato-emarginate in both sexes; and the light organs are wanting. In the ♂ the seventh ventral is broadly but angularly emarginate, and the eighth is obtuse and impressed or channeled : in the ♀ the last ventral is nicked at the tip, and a little smaller than the last dorsal. The form of body is elongate-oval, or sometimes rather broadly oval.

Broader oval, prothorax black and pale; elytra costate; ventral segments entirely black...2.

Elongate-oval; prothorax, last dorsal and last two ventral segments yellow. Length 8.5 mm. N. Mex.: Colo..**flavicollis** Lec.

2.—Antennal third joint but little longer than wide; elytra with obsolete costæ: prothorax with disc and margins black, remaining parts rosy and yellow. Length 12—16 mm. Vanc.; Or.: Cala.....................**californica** Motsch.

a.—Much smaller; 8.5 mm.: Or.

Antennal third joint longer than wide; elytra strongly costate: prothorax with disc and margins black, remaining parts rosy and yellow: varies greatly in size and form :' Atlantic slope.............................**corrusca** Fabr.

Type.—Moderately large and wide: size 13.5 by 6.4 and 9 by 4 mm. Mass.; Colo.: Va.

a.—Small and broad; ♀; size 7 by 4.7 mm.; *autumnalis* Mels.

β.—Small and narrow: ⚥ ♀; size 7.5 by 3 mm.; *lacustris* Lec.; (in one specimen from Slave Lake the elytral costæ are obsolete): L. Sup.; H. B. Terr.

PYROPYGA Motsch.

Antennæ rather wide, compressed, more or less serrate, second joint transverse, one-third as long as the third. Last dorsal ⚥ ♀ broadly truncate with rounded angles: segments lobed at the sides, with the angles but feebly produced backwards. Form elongate-oval, narrow, light organs inconspicuous except in *luteicollis.*

The specific distinctions are sometimes very indefinite, and depend on slight antennal characters as in *Plateros.*

A.—Antennæ broad, subserrate, third joint shorter than fourth : last dorsal and last two ventral segments yellow : last dorsal ⚥ almost rounded at tip.

Black, prothorax and scutel yellow, the former narrowed in front, apex acutely rounded. Length 8 mm. Fla.............................**luteicollis** Lec.

B.—Antennæ narrow, not serrate, third joint longer than fourth, last dorsal broadly truncate.

Prothorax with black disc and edges; elytra black..............................2.

Prothorax with black disc and reddish-yellow sides..............................3.

2.—Elytra costate; 6.5—8 mm.: Pa.? L. Sup.; Colo.; Cala...**fenestralis** Mels.

Elytra not costate; 4.5—6 mm.; Can.; Mass.: Pa. Va......**nigricans** Say.

3.—Elytra black; antennæ less slender, joints one-half longer than wide; 5—7 mm.; N. Y.; Tex.; Ariz.; Fla....................**decipiens** Harris.

Elytra black or piceous; antennæ narrower, joints twice as long as wide; 4 mm.; N. J.; Fla.............................**minuta** Lec.

Elytra piceous, with pale margin and narrow sutural line; 6—7 mm.; Detroit, Mich.; Lake Tahoe, Cala.............................**indicta** n. sp.

P. indicta.—Elongate, piceous, margins of ventral and pectoral segments paler; prothorax wider than long, nearly semicircular, apical and lateral margin pale, narrowly reflexed and punctured; hind angles acute; disc convex, feebly carinate, tinged with rosy each side, dorsal vitta dark, wide, somewhat dilated along the base, which is rectilinear. Scutel large, obtuse behind, blackish. Elytra opake, finely scabrous, with only obsolete costæ, side margin narrowly reflexed ; sides, tip and suture pale. Head black, eyes small in both sexes, front wide ; antennæ compressed, not serrate, second joint half as long as the third, which is equal to the fourth. Length 6—7 mm.

♂.—Lower joints of antennæ wider and diminishing more rapidly in width than in ♀; last dorsal segment truncate, obtusely triangular : seventh ventral emarginate, eighth narrower, obtuse at tip.

♀.—Antennæ narrower of more uniform width ; last dorsal obtusely triangular, truncate as in the ♂; seventh ventral slightly emarginate at tip.

Not uncommon at Detroit, where it was collected by Messrs. Hubbard and Schwarz ; a precisely similar specimen was taken by Mr. Bolter at Lake Tahoe, (alt. 6465'), California.

This insect has a deceptive resemblance to *Photinus consanguineus* and other species of that genus.

TENASPIS n. g.

Antennæ compressed, serrate, shorter in ♀ than ♂ : second joint one-half as long as third, which in the ♂ is shorter than the fourth. Head very small, prothorax feebly carinate in front. Dorsal segments strongly lobed and produced backwards at the sides : last dorsal segment in ♂ broadly emarginate with prominent rounded angles, in ♀ rounded at tip : seventh ventral in ♂ acutely emarginate, eighth small, narrow : last ventral of ♀ slightly nicked at tip. Light organs wanting. Form broadly oval.

Seems to differ from *Ilyas* by the antennæ not being pectinate, and by the light organs being entirely wanting.

Broadly oval, flat, black ; prothorax pale, tinged with rosy, dorsal stripe and hind angles blackish ; elytra acutely margined, each with two divergent elevated lines. Size 13 by 7 ; Texas and Northern Mexico..............**angularis** Gorham.

PYRACTOMENA Lec. (nec Motsch.)

Antennæ ♂ ♀ narrow, not serrate, shorter in ♀ ; prothorax subcari-nate, sides broadly reflexed, pale, tinged with rosy ; dorsal stripe and lateral cloud dusky ; elytra with suture and side margin pale. Light organs well developed in both sexes, larger in ♂ than ♀, situated in the fifth and sixth ventral segments, marked each side about one-half way between the middle and the side in the ♂ with a large stigma-like pore ;*

---

* This stigma-like pore, according to Dr. Hagen, is a muscular impression, caused by the insertion of a large band of fibres which run transversely outwards. The function of these muscles and their relation to the light organs are not yet under-stood, but next summer when living specimens can be obtained, renewed observa-tions will be made. Dr. Hagen thinks that these impressions can be traced, though less distinctly, in other genera of this family and also in Elateridæ. I have not yet been able to satisfy myself that such is the case, though doubtless the same muscles

♂ with last dorsal segment emarginate, seventh ventral truncate, and eighth small. The light organs in the ♀ are at the sides of the segments, which are dusky or piceous at the middle, and with distinct stigmatiform pores; the last dorsal and ventral are of usual form, presenting no peculiarities. This genus corresponds with *Pyrectosoma* Motsch., (Et. Ent. 1853, 38), but the specific name *versicolor*, which he attributes to the type, belongs to a species of *Photuris*.

Elytra with narrower side margin..2.

Elytra with wide side margin, surface opake, alutaceo-granulate, not punctured, discoidal costæ well marked: antennæ as long as prothorax; ventral segments ♀ testaceous, spotted with dusky; 7.5—12 mm.; Can.; Mass.; Ill.; Ga...1. **angulata** Say.

2.—Antennæ shorter than prothorax...3.

Antennæ longer than prothorax. ....4.

3.—Elytra not punctured, discoidal costæ well marked, abdomen ♀ in great part dark: 8.5—15 mm.; Me.; Mass.; Can.: L. Sup.; Tex.; Montana.
2. **borealis** Rand.

Elytra densely punctured, discoidal costæ obsolete; abdomen ♀ yellow, spotted with piceous; 14 mm.; Fla.....................................3. **nitidiventris** Lec.

4.—Narrower, ventral segments 1—4 piceous, seventh with a piceous spot; ♀ fifth and sixth piceous, with sides and hind margin yellow; light organs smaller than in the other species; 8.5—15 mm.: Mass.; Mich.: Pa.: Ga.; Tex.
4. **lucifera** Mels.

PHOTINUS Lap. emend. Lec. (nec Lacordaire).

This genus as emended by me (Pr. Ac. Nat. Sc. Phila. 1852, 334), differs from the preceding by the prothorax not at all carinate, but usually slightly channeled, and more obtusely rounded in front. The surface is pale, tinged with rosy, and is usually marked with a dusky spot or stripe. The light organs are always larger in the ♂ than in the ♀, and in the latter sex vary considerably according to species; in the ♂ they occupy the whole of the ventral segments from the fourth or fifth inclusive; on the fifth and sixth segments the stigmatiform impressions are very distinct, except in the division *Gynaptera*, where they are nearly obsolete; in the ♀ the light organs occupy the middle part of the ventral segments, and exhibit themselves mostly as a flat elevation on the fifth segment. The stigma-like impressions are barely or not visible in the ♀, which may thus be easily distinguished from the ♀ of the species of the preceding genus. Some of the species are among the most abundant and beautiful of our lightning bugs, though less gregarious than *Photuris*.

---

exist, but with a purely normal respiratory function. It may be affirmed with great probability, that these impressions are homologous with the ventral setigerous pores or foveæ of Carabidæ and Staphylinidæ, which bear the so called ambulatorial setæ. In Lampyridæ these foveæ are conspicuous only in this and the following genus (*Photinus*), so far as the genera occur in our fauna.

Fourth ventral segment dark: (PYRECTOSOMA *Motsch.*)..................................2.

Fourth ventral segment pale, at least in part..9.

2.—Prothorax with a black stripe and two roseate spots.........................3.

Prothorax with a large dusky cloud...5.

Prothorax with a black spot, sometimes wanting....................................6.

3.—Elytra with narrow side margin..4.

Elytra with wide side margin; ♀ with sixth ventral dark piceous; 8—11 mm.:
Mass.; Pa.; Va...**consanguineus** Lec.

   a.—Larger and broader than the type; sixth ventral of ♀ dark in front,
   yellow behind; 13 mm.; Ga.; Fla.

4.—Small and narrow, antennæ wider; ♀ with the usual transverse luminous
spot on the fifth ventral, and a much smaller round one on the sixth; rest
of ventral surface piceous: 4—6.5 mm.; Ga.; Fla.............**lineellus** Lec.

5.—Narrower than *consanguineus*; elytra with narrow side margin; antennæ narrow; fifth ventral of ♀ pale, with only a small lateral spot dark; sixth without luminous spot; 6—12.5 mm.; Mass.; L. Sup.; Kansas.....**ardens** Lec.

6.—Antennæ shorter and rather stouter than usual; prothorax channeled, very
obtusely rounded in front...7.

Antennæ of usual length; prothorax normally rounded in front................8.

7.—Smaller, prothoracic spot elongate, wider in front; apex and sides dusky,
strongly punctured; scutel dusky; ♂ with light organs as usual, fifth
ventral and following segments entirely luminous: ♀ light organs entirely
wanting: 5—7 mm.; Texas.................................**dimissus** n. sp.

Prothoracic spot transverse, apical, strongly punctured, sides punctured, scutel
yellow; ♂ with light organs as usual; ♀ unknown: 7 mm.; Fla.; Tex.
                                               collustrans Lec.

8.—Prothorax densely punctulate, apical part more strongly punctured, dusky,
sides dusky: ♀ unknown: 10—11.5 mm.; Ill.; Ks....**punctulatus** Lec.

Disc of prothorax smooth, convex, roseate, apex and sides strongly punctured;
elytra more strongly punctured: fifth ventral of ♀ with a transverse yellow boss occupying the middle third of the segment; 7 mm.; Fla.
                                               umbratus Lec.

9.—Large species, ventral impressions of ♂ very distinct, (ELLIPOLAMPIS *Motsch.*).10.

Small species, ventral impressions of ♂ obsolete..............................11.

10.—Prothorax not channeled, disc roseate without black spot; ♂ with hind
margin of fourth and the whole of the following ventral segments yellow;
♀ segments similarly colored, but the pale apical margin of the fourth is
very narrow: 14 mm.; Texas, (Boll.)........................**benignus** n. sp.

Prothorax with short dorsal channel, disc roseate with a large black spot;
♂ as in *benignus*; ♀ with dusky spots at the base of the fifth segment, sixth
dusky, margined with testaceous; 9—14 mm.; Pa.; Ill.; Tex...**pyralis** Linn.

   a.—Prothorax with a black vitta.

   β.—Prothorax without black spot: Tex.

11.—Elytra widely margined; ♀ with long elytra and wings, similar to the ♂;
6—8 mm.; Pa.; Va.; Tex...................................**marginellus** Lec.

   a.—Prothorax with a black vitta; Va.; Tex.

   β.—Paler, disc of prothorax roseate, without spot; Pa.; Ga.; *castus* Lec.

Elytra less widely margined; ♀ without wings, elytra short, dehiscent,
separately rounded at tip; 5.5—8 mm.; Mass.; Pa.; Ks.; (GYNAPTERA Lec.)
                                                scintillans Say.

Group 3.—Lampyres.

A sufficient character for separating this group is found in the last joint of the antennæ which is usually appendiculate, rarely (*Pleotomus*) sinuate near the tip. The joints of the antennæ vary in number as well as form. The sexes are dissimilar; the ♀ is frequently larviform with very short scale-like elytra; the light organs seem to be always brilliant in the ♀, but variable in the ♂, sometimes well developed (*Phausis reticulata*) sometimes wanting (*P. inaccensa*). The eyes of the ♂ are very large, contiguous or nearly so, both above and beneath. In the ♀ they are moderately large (*Pleotomus*) or very small (*Microphotus*).

Antennæ bipectinate, 14-jointed, very short and compact in the ♀; eyes moderately large in ♀, very large and nearly contiguous in ♂; ♀ with very short distant elytra,...**PLEOTOMUS.**

Antennæ simple, with quadrate joints: eleventh joint with an articulated acicular appendage; ♀ with short elytra; prothorax with transparent spots......**PHAUSIS.**

Antennæ short, simple, with quadrate joints: 9-jointed (♂), or 8-jointed (♀); eyes very large, contiguous (♂), very small, transverse, distant (♀): elytra of ♀ very short, rounded ....**MICROPHOTUS.**

PHAUSIS Lec.

This genus is not sufficiently distinct from the European *Lamprohiza* Motsch., and in fact the European species seems to have been naturalized in Maryland and Illinois. The last dorsal segment is deeply emarginate in the ♂, with acute angles; the transparent prothoracic spots are very distinct in ♂, but nearly wanting in ♀. The latter sex in *P. reticulata* has elytra about as long as in *Phot. scintillans.*

Fifth and sixth ventral segments yellow, luminiferous...............................2.

Ventral segments piceous, without light organs; elytra less strongly reticulate (♂); 6 mm.; Marquette, Lake Superior................................3. **inaccensa.**

2.—Prothorax wider than long, elytra densely punctured: (♂) 8.5 mm.; Md.; Ill.

1. **splendidula.**

Prothorax not wider than long, very obtuse in front, elytra confusedly reticulate, long in ♂, short in ♀; ♀ elytra short, not longer than metathorax: dehiscent, rounded at tip; 5.5 mm.; Ga.; Tenn.; Tex......2. **reticulata.**

MICROPHOTUS Lec.

The prothorax is very obtusely rounded in front, not carinate and without transparent spots; the elytra ♂ are somewhat dehiscent and rounded at tip; the discoidal costæ are distinct and the surface granulato-punctate. Antennæ very short in ♂, ten-jointed, not extending across the eyes which are prodigiously large; ♀ larviform, antennæ still shorter, nine-jointed, elytra small, distant, scale-like.

Body oval, elytra rounded on the sides: ♂ 6—10 mm.; ♀ unknown; Cape San Lucas, L. Cala...**dilatatus** Lec.

Body elongate, elytra with parallel sides; ♂ 6—10 mm.; ♀ 8—10 mm.; Cala.; Or.; Col..**angustus** Lec.

PLEOTOMUS Lec.

The development of this genus has been traced by Mrs. V. O. King, Austin, Texas; and the results of her observation are published in Psyche iii, 51—53. For a good series of specimens I am indebted to Mrs. King and Mr. Belfrage. I have separated the ♀ found by Mr. W. M. Davis in the mountains of Kentucky as a distinct species, on account of the much greater length of the prothorax; the ♂ is unfortunately unknown. The light organs are brilliant in the ♀, less so in the ♂. The prothorax is finely carinate and the elytral costæ distinct.

Prothorax not longer than wide, obtusely rounded in front; ♂ 11 mm.; ♀ 17 mm.; Texas..**pallens** Lec.
Prothorax nearly one-half longer than wide, sides obliquely converging, rather acutely rounded in front; ♀ 18 mm.; Cumberland Gap, Ky...**Davisii** n. sp.

As there is no other character available at present for the distinction of the second species, a longer description is unnecessary.

Group 4.—*Luciolæ.*

The eyes are large, convex and widely separated above and beneath in both sexes, not conspicuously larger in ♂; the head is rounded, narrowed behind and not retractile; it is but partially covered by the prothorax, which is, however, of the usual hood-like form and rounded in front. The antennæ are longer than one-half the body, filiform, slender, not compressed, inserted near the anterior margin of the front, and moderately approximate; the second and third joints are about equal, and together are as long as each of the following joints.

The sexes are similar in form with long elytra and well developed wings; the light organs occupy the whole of the fifth and following segments; stigma-like pores are not obvious, being situated at the base of the fifth and sixth segments and less strongly marked than in Pyractomena and Photinus ♂. The seventh ventral in ♀ is obtusely triangular; in ♂ the fifth and sixth are broadly emarginate, the seventh is smaller than in ♀, sinuate at the sides and prolonged at the middle, the eighth is a little wider and longer than the prolongation of the seventh. In our species the outer (or anterior) claw is cleft at tip. The prothorax and elytra are densely rugosely punctured, the former is yellow with a black stripe or spot, each side of which the disc is red; the latter have the whole margin and frequently a discoidal stripe pale. A single genus occurs in our fauna with limited representation.

PHOTURIS Lec.

Prothorax dull yellow, disc red, with a dark median stripe; head broadly not deeply concave; labrum tridentate; elytra with a pale discoidal stripe 10.5—15 mm.; N. Y.; Fla.; Ks...**pensylvanica.**
a.—Elytra dark, margined with pale, discoidal stripe absent.

Smaller and narrower, elytra more strongly punctured, head strongly concave. labrum not toothed; 10 mm.; Ga.; Fla.; Tex.................. ....**frontalis.**
Of same size and form as *frontalis;* prothorax with two dusky spots and a pale dorsal stripe; head more broadly concave; labrum indistinctly tridentate; 10 mm.: Ks...**divisa.**

Tribe 2.—PHENGODINI.

The prothorax though rounded in front does not cover the head, which is exposed. The eyes are convex, prominent, and widely separated; the antennæ are not approximate, inserted in front and inside of the eyes, and are plumose or flabellate in the ♂; (♀ unknown). The mandibles are long, slender and curved. the labrum connate with the front, small in Pterotus, large and emarginate in Phengodes; the middle coxæ are contiguous. the metasternum between them being narrowly carinate; the side pieces of metathorax are broad and diagonally divided. The gula is deeply impressed or excavated in all the genera.

Three subtribes are indicated :

Prosternum well developed in front of coxæ; front convex, narrowed between the antennæ...PTEROTINI.
Prosternum very short as usual; front flat, labrum large.. ....PHENGODINI.
Prosternum well developed; front convex, labrum small..............MASTINOCERINI.

PTEROTINI.

PTEROTUS Lec.

P. obscuripennis Lec.. from California; rufo-testaceous with piceous elytra; length 10—12 mm. The antennæ are long. inserted under two large convexities, ramose, the first joint stout, second small, 3—10 with long processes, that of the third being medial and that of the tenth apical ; eleventh as long as the process of the tenth, simple. Palpi short, joints oval, nearly equal. Tibiæ not compressed ; fourth joint of tarsi moderately dilated. somewhat bilobed ; ♂ seventh ventral broadly and deeply emarginate. eighth flat. narrower, obtuse ; last dorsal of similar size and form.

PHENGODINI.

The labrum is large ; metathoracic side pieces wide.
Elytra subulate, tarsi with fourth joint lobed... .... **PHENGODES.**
Elytra entire, tarsi with third and fourth joints lobed........ ....**ZARHIPIS.**

PHENGODES Latr.

The head is deeply transversely excavated behind the eyes; the gular region is also deeply excavated and the sutures are confluent.

The seventh ventral of the ♂ (the only sex known), is strongly emarginate. and the eighth narrower, obtuse at tip. The last dorsal is not emarginate. with sometimes the head and tips of elytra fuscous.

The species are testaceous in color and resemble each other very closely, but the prothoracic differences seem to warrant their reception as distinct.

Head testaceous, side margin of prothorax widely explanate behind, gradually narrowed in front..2.
Head fuscous...3.
2.—Front sparsely punctured, not channeled; vertex more deeply excavated, occiput channeled; 14 mm.; Tex.: (six specimens)..................**frontalis** n. sp.
Front and vertex with a distinct channel; occiput channeled: 12 mm.: N. Y.: (one specimen)...**plumosa** Oliv.
3.—Prothorax with the lateral margin very wide and not narrower in front: front strongly punctured: 17 mm.; N. Car.; (Dr. Horn) ....**laticollis** n. sp.
Prothorax with the lateral margin moderate, narrower in front; front sparsely punctured; 12 mm.; Tex.; (three specimens)..................**fusciceps** Lec.
Prothorax with the lateral margin narrow: 8.5 mm.: La.; (one specimen, Mr. Sallé)...**Sallei** n. sp.

I may add that the antennæ are shorter in the last two species, being less than half as long as the body, while in the others they are nearly two-thirds as long. As there are no other conspicuous differences than those mentioned in the table, longer descriptions are unnecessary, and would only mislead the student.

ZARHIPIS n. g.

This genus agrees with *Phengodes* in all respects except the following: The head is less deeply concave between the eyes, and not transversely constricted or impressed behind; epistome elevated above the labrum; the elytra are nearly as long as the abdomen, slightly dehiscent and rounded at tip; the third as well as the fourth tarsal joints are furnished beneath with a distinct membranous sole; the seventh ventral is acutely emarginate; the sixth segment is also emarginate, but the seventh is cleft almost to the base, and the lobes sometimes overlap behind presenting the appearance of a narrow closed slit, in which the basal part of the eighth ventral is visible.

Three species from California are known to me:

Prothorax with side margin strongly reflexed...............,....................... ....2.
Prothorax with narrow side margin..3.
2.—Blackish piceous, mandibles and prothorax bright rufo-testaceous; base of antennæ and scutel reddish, legs tinged with red: prothorax more strongly margined, and antennæ stouter than in *integripennis;* 13.5 mm.; Cala.; (Hardy, one specimen)...................................... ....**ruficollis** n. sp.
Shining rufo-testaceous, elytra piceous, densely rugosely punctulate, antennæ dark, with the base pale: 10—13 mm.: Cala.........**integripennis** Lec.
3.—Exactly like *integripennis* except that the prothorax is more convex, with narrow side margin, and the head behind the eyes under surface of the body are piceous, the legs and scutel are however yellow; 10 mm.: Berkeley, Cala.: Mr. J. J. Rivers, (one specimen)..................**piciventris** n. sp.

MASTINOCERINI.

These are small, slender insects, having the antennæ biramose, or serrate but not flabellate as in Phengodini, the branches being less slender. The eyes are small, lateral and convex ; the epistome is somewhat convex, and the labrum is small and indistinct ; the mandibles are acute but not prominent. The maxillary palpi are long, the labial very short ; the gula is less deeply excavated than in *Phengodes*. The side pieces of metathorax are long and narrow, diagonally divided, with the epimera exposed. The elytra are short, dehiscent, and rounded at tip.

Antennæ ramose.

Lateral margin of prothorax acute ; palpi broad.............**MASTINOCERUS.**

Lateral margin of prothorax obliterated in front : palpi slender...**CENOPHENGUS.**

Antennæ serrate...**TYTTHONYX.**

MASTINOCERUS Solier.

In this genus the labrum is small and indistinct, and the epistome slightly convex, more advanced than in the two preceding genera : the head between the eyes is flattened, scarcely concave : the gula is much less excavated, and the maxillary palpi are long, flattened, not slender, with the last joint triangular or rather securiform. The antennæ are not longer than the head, biramose, with the branches shorter and stouter, though still flexible. The eyes are lateral, moderately large and convex. The flanks of the prothorax are acutely margined, flat, not concave, the edge of the disc is not margined nor flattened. The metasternum is longer than usual, with narrow side pieces, but the epimera are large. The elytra are less than one-half as long as the abdomen ; dehiscent and rounded at tip, without distinct epipleuræ. Legs slightly compressed ; joints 1—4 of tarsi gradually a little shorter and narrower, fourth small, not lobed beneath.

♂ .—Seventh ventral deeply emarginate ; eighth prominent, obtuse.

Elongate, uniformly punctured, pubescent, testaceous, abdomen darker, with the last two segments paler: (♀ unknown); ♂ 6 mm.; Texas.............**texanus.**

 a.—Piceous, head prothorax, legs and last ventral segment dark red.

I am also indebted to Mrs. King for a larva of *Mastinocerus*, of slender, cylindrical form and pale color. It was feebly luminous, and lived upon small snails. The perfect insect is thus mentioned in a letter, the observations being made upon a specimen attracted by the lamp : "June 4th saw running rapidly over the table near a lighted lamp, a small Coleopter ; it was twisting its abdomen up over its wings, and evidently trying to straighten them out, as they seemed moist and twisted at their ends. The general appearance suggested *Mastinocerus*, and acting on this thought, I captured it and sat up till a late hour to be assured of the truth. The insect was in a small vial and moved quickly. It gave out light conspicuously from the head, feebly from the anal end, and still more so from about the base of the abdomen. The light seen in the head, though visible in the dark as a round spot, yet when taken into a room obscurely lighted was invisible from above; but when the insect was suddenly thrown upon its back a light no larger than a pin point was seen just about the junction of the head and prothorax."

CENOPHENGUS n. g.

I have established this new genus upon a small Californian species, which greatly resembles in appearance *Mastinocerus texanus*, but differs by the antennæ as long as the head and prothorax; the prothorax a little longer than wide, with the lateral edge distinct only behind the middle, and quite obliterated in front. The maxillary palpi are elongate and slender, with the last joint long and cylindrical. The seventh ventral segment is more broadly emarginate, and the eighth comparatively larger. In all other respects it closely resembles *M. texanus*, except that the sculpture is finer.

C. debilis.—Elongate, blackish piceous, punctulate and pubescent. Prothorax not as wide as the head, longer than wide, disc flattened towards the base, apex truncate, sides parallel, base and hind angles strongly rounded; testaceous, piceous near the base. Elytra flattened, half as long as the abdomen, finely scabrous-punctate, sides somewhat rounded with a submarginal elevated line from before the middle nearly to the tip. Legs and last segment tinged with testaceous. Length 4.5 mm.

California; two specimens; Dr. Horn. The second and third joints of the antennæ are short and without branches; the branches of the other joints are from one and a half to twice as long as the joints; in *Mastinocerus* they are about four times longer than the joints; ♀ unknown.

TYTTHONYX Lec.

The well-known but not abundant species which is the type of this genus, is of somewhat difficult location. Its appearance would indicate a relationship with the Malthini group of Telephoridae, but after a careful study of its characters I am inclined to believe that its true position is near *Mastinocerus* and *Cenophengus*, with perhaps a closer tendency towards *Drilus* than is exhibited in those genera.

The characters have been sufficiently given by me in other places to permit of the easy recognition of this genus, but in order to substantiate the opinion above expressed it is now necessary to go into greater details.

Head broader than long, deflexed, eyes small, rounded, convex, prominent, finely granulated; epistome rounded in front, connate with the labrum and covering the mandibles which are curved, slender at tip, broadly toothed about the middle ; palpi with the last joint oval, obliquely truncate. so as to appear pointed and aciculate at tip; ligula and mentum small, supported on a broad gular peduncle which is concavely impressed behind; sutures widely separated. Antennæ long, broadly compressed, strongly serrate, joints triangular, second but one-half as long and one-half as wide as the third, outer joints (♂) longer, narrower and more prolonged at tip than the lower joints. Prothorax transverse, truncate in front, broadly rounded behind, sides short, inflexed flanks very narrow ; under surface of prothorax membranous, with the exception of a very very narrow collar which supports the front legs; coxæ and trochantins large. Middle coxæ contiguous. Side pieces of metathorax broad, narrowed and pointed behind, not sinuate on the inner margin, epimera exposed. Elytra one-half as long as the abdomen, rounded at tip ; epipleuræ narrow, but distinct for one-half the length. Scutel broad, slightly emarginate behind. Wings straight, extending along the dorsal surface of the abdomen. Legs feeble, claws small, simple.

♂ .—Antennæ nearly as long as the body, strongly serrate, seventh ventral segment broadly emarginate. eighth narrow, channeled.

♀ .—Antennæ two-thirds as long as the body, outer joints narrower, but not longer than the lower joints.

Black, opake. sparsely and finely pubescent, front, occiput and under surface of head fulvous. Length 4 mm.; Middle States, on leaves.

erythrocephalus Fabr.

Sub-family III.—TELEPHORIDÆ.

The insects of this sub-family are closely related to the Lampyridæ genuini. but are easily known by the stronger development of the mouth organs, the smaller size of the eyes, which permits the antennæ to be widely separated at the base, and by the straight, or nearly straight outline of the inner side of the metathoracic episterna.

Light organs do not exist in any of the species, and the sexes are very similar in form, differing, at most, by the length of the antennæ and the outline of the sides of the prothorax. Sexual characters are also seen in the last segments of the abdomen, especially in *Chauliognathus* and *Malthodes ;* in the latter genus the claspers assume large size and great complexity. In a few instances tibial and tarsal characters distinguish the sexes, and in many species of *Telephorus* the ungues are quite different.

I have excluded the singular genus *Omethes* from this sub-family. It is not a Lampyride. but where it may be suitably placed I do not know.

Two tribes may be recognized in our fauna :

Mentum very long, wider in front................................CHAULIOGNATHINI.
Mentum small. quadrate.................................TELEPHORINI.

Tribe 1.—CHAULIOGNATHINI.

This tribe consists of but one genus represented in our fauna by a moderate number of species. They are much more numerous in Tropical America, but so far as I am aware do not occur in other countries.

CHAULIOGNATHUS Hentz.

This genus differs from all others in our fauna not only by the elongated head, and singular structure of the maxillary lobe which has a long extensile and contractile fleshy filament, but also by the peculiar arrangement of the under surface of the prothorax, and the sexual characters of the ♂.

The prosternum is but feebly developed, and separated by membrane from the surrounding parts. The trochantin is very large, triangular and flat, and the inflexed flanks wide and concave; the two gular plates at the anterior margin of the prosternum are large and prominent, dipping perpendicularly inwards. The mentum is very long and narrow, a little broader in front; the gular sutures run from the hind angles of the mentum obliquely inwards, and coalesce on the median line, almost to the hind margin of the lower floor of the cranium.

The last ventral segment of the ♂ is elongate-oval, convex, and of firmer corneous consistency than the other segments; the penultimate ventral is emarginated broadly and deeply by the convexity of the last segment; from the terminal opening between the last ventral and dorsal is frequently seen protruding a pair of claspers, of slender curved form, hooked at the end and fringed on the inner margin with spines, thus resembling the inner lobe of the maxillæ of Carabidæ.

These characters and those already given by me in the Classification (p. 186), abundantly indicate the propriety of recognizing this type as a separate tribe.

In several species the antennæ in the ♂ are longer than in the ♀, and the outer joints are somewhat broader; but there is not sufficient difference in this respect to be worth indicating among the specific characters in the table.

Antennæ slender in both sexes.
Antennæ with third joint equal, or nearly so, to fourth...............................2.
Antennæ with third joint conspicuously shorter than the fourth.....................5.
2.—Head yellow; prothorax opake.. 3.
    Head black; prothorax shining...................... ....4.
3.—Prothorax wider than long, sides very broadly and strongly reflexed; red, finely pubescent; mouth organs, three prothoracic dots, abdominal spots and last segments, legs, except at base, and posterior one-fourth to one-fifth of elytra black; antennæ testaceous and dusky, scape black. Length 13—17 mm.: Arizona..1. **profundus.**

Prothorax longer than wide, nearly elliptical, sides narrower and strongly reflexed: ochreous, finely pubescent; antennæ, mouth organs, two prothoracic spots and a medial oval fovea, legs and abdominal spots black; elytra punctured, each with a small black spot behind the middle, which is frequently wanting. Length 11—14 mm.; Texas...............2. **discus.**

4.— Black, prothorax and elytra yellow; the former wider than long, sides strongly and widely reflexed: disc with an angulated black transverse spot: scutel black: elytra punctured, with a black basal spot, and another behind the middle, extending from the side almost to the suture; sixth and seventh abdominal segments above and below spotted with black. Length 10—12 mm.: Utah.....................3. **fasciatus** n. sp.

5.— Elytra with a large apical black spot, not margined with yellow...............6.
Elytra with the entire margin yellow......................7.

6.— Disc of prothorax opake black, margined with yellow; elytra with part of suture and sometimes triangular common basal spot, abdomen (♀) yellow, last segments spotted with black. Length 11 mm.: Texas: N. Mex.; Col. 4. **limbicollis.**

Disc of prothorax smooth, shining yellow, with a large black spot, sometimes reduced to three small dots: abdomen yellow, banded and spotted with black in ♀; last segment only dusky or black in ♂, and finely sparsely punctulate. Length 9—11 mm.; Col.; Utah.....................5. **basalis.**

7.—Antennæ with third joint more than twice as long as second; head entirely black.................................9.

Antennæ with third joint twice as long as second; head yellow with black spots..........................12.

9.—Elytra with basal black spot......................10.
Elytra with base entirely yellow.....................11.

10.—Basal spot of elytra triangular: posterior spot one-half the length of the elytra. Length 9—13 mm.; Texas....................6. **scutellaris.**
Basal spot of elytra transverse: posterior spot three-fourths the length of the elytra. Length 9 mm.; New Mexico.................7. **Lewisii.**

11. —Prothorax not wider than long, disc opake black, narrowly margined with yellow, sides more narrowly reflexed. Length 10 mm.: Ariz...8. **opacus.**
Prothorax wider than long, margin more widely reflexed, opake yellow, with a transverse discoidal spot: elytra with a black spot, which is sometimes small and posterior, and sometimes covers nearly the whole surface. Length 9—11 mm.: N. Y.; Mo.; Ga.: Tex.....................9. **pensylvanicus.**

12.--Prothorax longer than wide, opake yellow, with a broad black dorsal stripe, sides very narrowly margined: elytra with discoidal spot sometimes extending nearly the whole length, sometimes wanting. Length 8—11 mm.: N. Y.: Fla. ....10. **marginatus.**

Tribe 2.—TELEPHORINI.

Excluding *Omethes* as above indicated, I have no improvement to suggest to the table of groups I have already given. Classification p. 187 :

Elytra covering the wings: gular sutures confluent: prothorax truncate in front: head entirely exposed...........................*Podabri.*
Elytra covering the wings: gular sutures separate: prothorax rounded in front: head partly covered..........................*Telephori.*
Elytra abbreviated, wings exposed: gular sutures confluent...........*Malthini.*

Group 1.—*Podabri.*

Although as will be seen below, the species of this group differ in the form of palpi, as well as in the tarsal claws, they seem to me to indicate but one natural genus. They are more numerous in the northern part of the Continent, and gradually fade out towards the tropics.

PODABRUS Westwood.

In this genus the gular sutures are confluent at the median line, and the head is prolonged and narrowed behind the eyes, so as to form a distinct neck not covered by the prothorax, which is nearly truncate, or even somewhat emarginate in front. The seventh ventral segment of the ♂ is truncate, and the eighth is exposed, sometimes triangular, sometimes with parallel sides and obtusely rounded at tip. The seventh ventral of the ♀ is triangular, subsinuate each side near the tip, which is frequently slightly nicked, though I have not found use for this character as a specific distinction, since from the drying of the specimens it is difficult to observe. The three divisions are so different as almost to entitle them to rank as distinct genera, though some forms link them together rather closely.

Claws armed with a long acute tooth, causing them to appear broadly cleft; maxillary palpi with last joint triangular; front tibiæ of ♂ more or less sinuate in form...**A.**

Claws armed with a broad nearly rectangular basal tooth; maxillary palpi with last joint elongate, slightly triangular, the inner and apical margin being rounded together...**B.**

Claws with a slender tooth nearly as long as the upper part and approximate to it, causing them to appear narrowly cleft..**C.**

A.—BRACHYNOTUS Kirby.

Eighth ventral ♂ triangular, flat, rounded at tip...2.

Eighth ventral ♂ parallel, obtusely rounded at tip......................................8.

2.—Last joint of maxillary palpi with apical side oblique, angle distinct, eyes prominent...3.

Last joint of maxillary palpi nearly transversely truncate, eyes small; black, mouth part of first joint of antennæ and sides of prothorax yellow; the latter much wider than long, rounded on the sides and broadly margined; head densely punctured, prothorax punctulate, elytra finely rugose; ♂ with front tibiæ dilated inwards into a thin plate. Length 7—10 mm.; Cala.

1. latimanus Motsch.

a.—Upper surface dull yellow, occiput and disc of prothorax piceous.

Last joint of maxillary palpi with the apical side very oblique, inner angle rounded, indistinct; eyes small; black, opake, finely pruinose with pubescence; sides of prothorax pale; head coarsely punctured, prothorax sparsely punctulate, much wider than long, rounded and explanate at the sides, dorsal line long and deep; elytra less finely rugose, with the side margin sometimes pale; ♀ antennæ scarcely half as long as the body, joints 2—4 slightly increasing in length; ♂ antennæ three-fourths as long as the body, second joint one-half as long as the third; seventh ventral slightly channeled, eighth triangular, obtusely rounded at tip. Length 8—9 mm.; Mass.; L. Superior.. 2. **nothoides** n. sp.

3.—Antennæ stouter; elytra distinctly dilated on the sides, elevated lines strongly marked...4.

Antennæ more slender, elytra not or scarcely dilated on the sides, elevated lines indistinct...5.

4.—Elytra very broadly dilated, densely rugose, opake; black, front and sides of prothorax pale; head and middle of prothorax densely punctured, the latter near three times wider than long, sides very broadly explanate and reflexed, dorsal line feeble; antennæ scarcely longer than half the body, joints 2—4 increasing in length; ♂ elytra less dilated on the sides, antennæ longer than in ♀. Length 11 —13 mm.; Can.; Pa...3. **tricostatus** Say.

Elytra less broadly dilated, densely rugose, opake; front and lateral margin of prothorax yellow; head coarsely, prothorax less coarsely punctured, not much wider than long, narrower in front, apex truncato-emarginate with the angles subacute, side margin deeply impressed before and behind, dorsal line well marked; joints of antennæ 2—4 increasing in length. Length 7—8 mm.; Mass.; N. Y.; L. Sup.; Ks.........................4. **rugosulus** Lec.

Very similar to *rugosulus*; prothorax less narrowed in front, with the apex truncate and angles rounded, disc less punctured, elytra less densely rugose and less opake, less dilated on the sides; ♂ wanting. Length 8—10 mm.; Va.; Ga.; Fla..5. **frater** Lec.

5.—Elytra rather coarsely rugose ....6.

Elytra more finely rugose..7.

6.—Color variable, front sometimes and margins of elytra pale; head coarsely punctured; prothorax twice wider than long, sides rounded, broadly explanate, yellow, with a large dark spot, disc sparsely punctured, dorsal line distinct; antennæ and legs more or less testaceous. Length 8—13 mm.; Atlantic region; Kansas..............................6. **basillaris** Say.

α.—Prothorax pale yellow, without spot, *flavicollis* Lec.

β.—Prothorax with a spot, legs testaceous, *discoideus* Lec.

γ.—Smaller, prothorax less strongly punctured, Kansas: *punctulatus* Lec.

Similar to *basilaris*, but prothorax scarcely longer than wide, with nearly parallel sides, rounded only near the tip, and narrower more strongly reflexed side margin; piceous, base of antennæ and mandibles, prothorax and margins of elytra pale. Length 9—11 mm......7. **quadratus** n. sp.

α.—Head entirely black, prothorax dusky; Texas: (Belfrage).

Piceous, frontal fascia, sides of prothorax and margins of elytra pale; head coarsely punctured behind; prothorax not much wider than long, sides nearly parallel, widely explanate, disc red, coarsely and densely punctured, dorsal line short, not very plain; claws more slender and more nearly cleft than in the foregoing species. Length 9 mm.; Fla.: one specimen, (Bolter)..8. **fissus** n. sp.

7.—Prothorax wider than long, feebly punctured in front, sides yellow, widely explanate; head not deeply punctured behind, front more or less pale; rest of body black, base of antennæ sometimes tinged with testaceous, dorsal line usually feeble. Length 9—11 mm.; Atlantic region; L. Sup.

9. **diadema** Fabr.

α.—Prothorax with the disc but little darker than the sides.

Very similar to *diadema*, but the antennæ and legs are yellow, or nearly so, and the margins of the elytra pale; the dorsal line of the prothorax is obsolete, and the discoidal convexities less prominent. Length 9—11 mm.; L. Sup.; Penn.; Ga..10. **modestus** Say.

Color mostly yellow above, piceous beneath; head punctured behind, prothorax smooth and shining, wider than long, sides widely explanate, parallel, rounded in front; discoidal convexities dark, dorsal line short; elytra tinged with piceous behind; antennæ and legs yellow; specimens will doubtless occur with the elytra dark colored, without pale margins. This species differs from the two preceding by the less transverse prothorax, with less rounded sides, and disc not at all punctured in front. Length 10 mm.; Cala.; San Mateo....................................11. **binotatus** n. sp.

8.—Head suddenly narrowed behind the eyes, neck short; prothorax wider than long...9.

Head much prolonged behind the eyes, neck long; prothorax not wider than long...10.

9.—Head, prothorax and margin of posterior ventral segments yellow; occiput sometimes dark, elytra black, with pruinose pubescence. Length 10—12 mm.; Cala.; Or.; Montana. .... 12. **comes** Lec.

a.—Body above yellow, elytra blackish behind : *gradatus* Lec.

Head, prothorax, abdominal margin, and legs yellow, antennæ dusky. yellow at the base; elytra black with pruinose pubescence. Length 9—12 mm.; Ill.; Cal ....13. **tomentosus** Say.

a.—Elytral margins pale.

10.—Head sparsely punctured behind, prothorax feebly punctured, dorsal line deep; yellow, elytra black, coarsely rugose, abdomen more or less piceous. Length 11—14 mm.; Conn.; Ohio; Penn. ....14. **protensus** Lec.

a.—Elytra yellow, gradually blackish behind : *protensus* Lec.

Head and prothorax coarsely punctured, dorsal line deep; front sides of prothorax, margins of elytra, legs, and base of antennæ yellow. Length 7—10 mm.; Penn.; Ga.; Ill.; Tex.....................15. **poricollis** Lec.

a.—Prothorax entirely yellow or brown : *brunnicollis* Lec.

B.—Malthaces Kirby.

Muzzle broad in front of the eyes; head coarsely punctured; fourth tarsal joint slightly emarginate..2.

Muzzle short; fourth tarsal joint slightly emarginate.................7.

Fourth tarsal joint deeply bilobed...............................14.

2.—Prothorax densely punctured, opake ....3.

Prothorax sparsely finely punctured...............................6.

3.—Dorsal line of prothorax feeble, convexities slight................4.

Dorsal line deep, convexities prominent...........................5.

4.—Black, prothorax with lateral spot red, sides slightly sinuate. Length 11 mm.; Or.; Vanc ....16. **scaber** Lec.

Piceous, anterior half of head, base of antennæ and margins of elytra pale; prothorax ferruginous, narrower behind, sides repand. Length 11 mm.; Penn.; Horn. ....17. **cinctipennis** Lec.

5.—Piceous, anterior half of head, sides of prothorax and margins of elytra pale; prothorax not wider than long, narrower behind, sides sinuate. Length 9 mm.; N. H.; (Austin, Blanchard)...............18. **limbellus** n. sp.

Black, anterior half of head, and prothorax red; prothorax not wider than long, narrowed behind, sides sinuate. Length 6—8 mm.; Can.: L. Sup.; Penn..19. **punctatus** Lec.

6.—Black, prothorax square, front angles rounded; very slightly punctulate, shining, dorsal line deep, sides more or less yellow; sides of muzzle testaceous; ♀ antennæ shorter, abdomen when distended longer than elytra. Length 8—10 mm.; Utah: Mont.: Col.; B. Col..................20. **brevipennis** Lec.

Piceous, base of antennæ, sides of mouth, sides of prothorax, and margins of elytra testaceous: head sparsely punctured behind, prothorax deeply concave at the middle, dorsal line fine, surface shining, sparsely punctulate. Length 8 mm.; L. Sup.; Mt. Wash., N. II., (Austin)....21. **puncticollis** Kirby.

7.—Head and prothorax finely punctured or punctulate; the latter with a wide medial concavity and two elongate convexities............... ....8.

Head nearly smooth; prothorax quite smooth..13.

8.—Prothorax shining, sparsely punctured, head finely punctured.................9.

Prothorax opake, punctulate, head punctulate...... ... .10.

9.—Black, prothorax not longer than wide, yellow, sides rounded near the apex; second joint of antennæ shorter than the third. Length 8 mm.; Cal., Lake Tahoe...22. **xanthoderus** n. sp.

a.—Prothorax with a broad black dorsal stripe; (perhaps distinct); B. Col.

Yellow, under surface and antennæ piceous, the latter yellow at base; prothorax much narrower than the head, longer than wide, sides parallel, slightly rounded in front, lateral basal impressions deeper and more defined; second joint of antennæ as long as the third. This species has a very deceptive resemblance to *cavicollis*, but is easily recognized by the different form of the tarsal claws. Length 6—9 mm.; Vanc.; Cal.; Nev.
23. **lutosus** n. sp.

10.—Prothorax longer than wide..11.

Prothorax not longer than wide...12.

11.—Prothorax with the sides fulvous, front angles very slightly obliquely truncate; head finely and densely punctured. Length 8 mm.; Cal.: San Mateo; one specimen ....24. **maeer** Lec.

Prothorax entirely black, front angles strongly obliquely truncate, base of antennæ dull testaceous: head not densely punctulate. Length 6—8 mm.; Can.; Mont.; Or.; Alaska, Vanc.................25. **piniphilus** Mann.

Head sparsely punctulate; Sitka, one specimen; (perhaps a distinct species).

12.—Anterior half of head and sides of prothorax yellow; head densely punctulate, tarsi moderately broad, especially the front pair. Length 7 mm.; Col.; N. Mex..............:...26. **lateralis** Lec.

a.—Prothorax entirely yellow.

Mouth piceous, three joints of antennæ and palpi testaceous, legs tinged with testaceous, head less distinctly punctured; Length 6 mm.; L. Sup.
27. **puberulus** Lec.

a.—Prothorax bright red: Canada.

Anterior half of head dull testaceous: base of antennæ and legs tinged with testaceous: prothorax with front angles strongly obliquely truncate, disc finely punctulate, less concave at the middle than in the preceding species; elytra more distinctly rugose-punctulate (as in *lateralis*), with indistinct elevated lines; side margin pale. Length 7 mm.; H. B. Terr.; one specimen...28. **extremus** n. sp.

Mouth, base of antennæ and prothorax yellow; the latter deeply concave at the middle, and finely punctulate, legs more or less testaceous. Length 5 mm.; Can.; Fla., (Bolter)..................................29. **simplex** Couper.

13.—Piceous, legs, front part of head and base of antennæ dull testaceous, prothorax not wider than long, somewhat narrower than the head. Length 6 mm.; N. H.; Can.; L. Sup.............................30. **lævicollis** Kirby.

14.—Muzzle broad, head less narrowed behind, finely punctulate; fourth tarsal joint deeply bilobed. Yellow above, head behind the eyes and under surface piceous; antennæ piceous, base yellow; palpi yellow, dark at tip; hind margin of elytra and tarsi piceous; prothorax feebly punctulate, not longer than wide, posterior concavity broad and deep, convexities narrow, prominent. Length 7.5 mm.; Cal., Tejon : one specimen.....33. **tejonicus** Lec.

Muzzle short, head less narrowed behind, smooth; fourth tarsal joint deeply bilobed. Black, mandibles and palpi pale, piceous at tip; prothorax very smooth and shining, somewhat wider than long, posterior concavity deep, convexities prominent, oval, bright yellow, apical and basal margin black. Length 6 mm.; Penn.; Can..32. **Pattoni** Lec.

Muzzle short; form very elongate, head not opake, strongly narrowed behind, sparsely punctured, eyes prominent; fourth tarsal joint deeply bilobed. Black, mandibles and sides of prothorax reddish-yellow; the latter longer than wide, indistinctly punctulate, sides parallel, front angles obliquely truncate, posterior concavity deep and large, convexities narrow, prominent. Very closely resembles *macer*, but the head is not densely punctured, and the fourth tarsal joint is quite different, being deeply bilobed. Length 6.5 mm.; Cal., Lake Tahoe; one specimen, (Bolter) .....31. **Bolteri** n. sp.

C.

The three species in this division are similar in appearance, being very slender, yellow above, piceous beneath, with the legs and base of antennæ yellow; the head is blackish behind the eyes and very much narrowed; the eyes are prominent. The last joint of the maxillary palpi is rather large, triangular, moderately dilated, with the distal side rounded and the inner angle not well defined. The tarsi are long and slender, the front pair stouter in *corneus;* the claws cleft at the tip, with the lower point as acute and nearly or quite as long as the upper. Prothorax sparsely punctured, small, not wider than long, deeply excavated, with elongate convexities.

Fourth tarsal joint deeply bilobed..2.

Fourth tarsal joint slightly emarginate; head strongly, not very densely punctured; prothorax sparsely punctured with the sides rounded in front; antennæ with the second and third joints equal, each scarcely shorter than the fourth; elytra finely rugose, piceous at tip; base of thighs and tarsi piceous; outer claw of hind tarsi toothed, all the others cleft; ♂ ♀. Length 9 mm.; Cal., Geyser, (Bolter); Nev., (Horn)..............34. **mellitus** n. sp.

2.—Head strongly, more densely punctured; prothorax nearly smooth, sides more broadly rounded in front; antennæ piceous, with second, third and fourth joint gradually increasing in length; elytra blackish at tip; legs piceous, tinged with testaceous; ♂. Length 9 mm.; Cal.; two ♂ ...35. **corneus** Lec.

Head very sparsely punctured; prothorax strongly punctured, much more deeply excavated at the middle, excavation blackish, convexities elongate, acute, region of hind angles also deeply excavated; antennæ with second, third and fourth joints nearly equal: ♂ ♀. Length 6 mm.; Cal., San Francisco: Nev., (Horn).....................................36. **cavicollis** Lec.

Group 2.—Telephori.

I find no reason for changing the table of genera previously given by me,* except to suppress *Rhagonycha*, which seems an unnecessary disintegration of Telephorus; our genera will then be as follows:

Last joint of maxillary palpi dilated, securiform..2.
Last joint of maxillary palpi suboval, obliquely truncate............................4.
  Hind angles of prothorax rounded ....3.
  Hind angles of prothorax (♂) incised; head short..........................**SILIS.**
3.—Head moderately long, sides of prothorax not incised............**TELEPHORUS.**
  Head short and broad, sides of prothorax (♂) nicked at the middle.
                                                                      POLEMIUS.
4.—Sides of prothorax (♂) incised at the middle and behind, antennæ (♂) strongly serrate ....**DITEMNUS.**

One species of the last named genus has recently occurred in California; with the exception of *Polemius*, they are therefore represented on both sides of the continent.

TELEPHORUS DeGeer.

The numerous species of this genus present at times sexual differences in the form of the prothorax and the tarsal claws, which render the distinction of species somewhat uncertain. They are likewise of variable color and soft texture, so that in dried specimens the form cannot be accurately defined. The present table may therefore be considered, while an improvement upon the crude work of my first synopsis,† only as a guide to observations in which by a good series of specimens being collected from the same locality and tree, the limits of variation may be more accurately determined.

The species in our fauna may be divided into the following groups:
Claws similar, all being toothed or cleft ....2.
Claws dissimilar, some being usually simple...3.
Claws simple or slightly broader at base ....4.
2.—All the claws appendiculate or broadly toothed...**A.**
  All the claws cleft or acutely toothed...**B.**
3.—Claws of front tarsi cleft, of middle and hind tarsi broadly toothed............**C.**
  Anterior claw of all the tarsi toothed at base, entire at tip............................**D.**
  Anterior claw of all the tarsi toothed at base, cleft at tip, elytra sparsely tuberculate ....**E.**
4.—Elytra tuberculate as in E ....**F.**
  Elytra finely scabrous ....**G.**

* Classification, 189.   † Proc. Acad. Nat. Sci. 1851, 339.

A.

Prothorax wider than long, but little rounded in front, and almost truncate; last joint of maxillary palpi dilated, triangular, inner angle well defined..........2.

Prothorax quadrate, but little rounded in front, and almost truncate; last joint of maxillary palpi elongate triangular, inner angle indistinct......................3.

2.—Dusky black, pruinose with gray pubescence; mouth and side margins of ventral segments testaceous; head and elytra very densely punctured; prothorax twice as wide as long, coarsely punctured, testaceous with an angulated piceous transverse spot; impressed dorsal line distinct. Length 8—9 mm.; N. Y.; Tex..1. **deutiger** Lec.

· a.—Side margin of elytra pale.

3.—Black, prothorax nearly smooth, narrowed in front, sides straight, margined, excavated about the middle, fulvous, with a dorsal black stripe; head densely finely punctured. ♀. prothorax wider and less excavated at the sides than in ♂. Length 5—5.5 mm.; N. Y.; Ill.; Fla............2. **excavatus** Lec.

a.—Side margin of elytra pale; tibiæ and tarsi sometimes testaceous; *marginellus* Lec.

β.—Prothorax yellow, without dorsal stripe.

Prothorax slightly broader than long, yellow, with narrow dorsal black stripe, sides straight, more finely margined, only slightly explanate in front of the middle; head opake, prothorax alutaceous; black, base of antennæ, palpi and part of legs testaceous; ♀. Length 4 mm.; N. Y.........3. **vilis** Lec.

Head opake, finely punctured; black, anterior half of head, mouth organs, base of antennæ and legs yellow; prothorax a little wider than long, sides nearly straight, narrowly margined, more strongly in front of middle, sparsely finely punctulate, yellow, with a narrow black dorsal stripe; ♀. Ill.; one specimen, (Bolter)..4. **pusio** n. sp.

Head shining, sparsely punctulate; prothorax ♂ as in *excavatus*; side margin of elytra, front half of head, base of antennæ and legs yellow; ♀. Prothorax a little wider than long, less excavated at the sides, and not impressed behind the middle. Length 5 -5.5 mm.; Ill.. (B. D. Walsh)...5. **Walshii** n. sp.

Black, mandibles and base of antennæ usually pale, tibiæ and tarsi tinged with testaceous, head punctulate, prothorax smooth, a little wider than long. Length 5—5.5 mm.; L. Sup.; Col.; Cal.; Alaska............6. **fraxini** Say.

B.

Moderate sized or small species, prothorax not elongate...........................2.

Small species, prothorax longer than wide ....7.

Larger, black, prothorax pale, broader than long, shining, with a large black discoidal spot; head sparsely punctulate, shining, anterior half and under side of first three antennal joints pale; palpi piceous, last joint dilated, strongly triangular; tarsi broad; ♂ tarsi broader than in ♀. Length 9—10 mm.; Can.; L. Sup.; Ill.; Penna................7. **carolinus** Fabr.

a.—The black parts are brown. *jactatus* Say ; Ks.

2.—Elytra more finely or sparsely rugose-punctured...........................3.

Elytra more coarsely and densely rugose-punctured; black, prothorax yellow with a wide dorsal stripe black, wider than long, side margin strongly reflexed, equally wide for the whole length; mouth sometimes piceo-testaceous. Length 3.5 -6 mm.; Atlantic region; Can.; Tex.; Fla.; N. Y.

s. **lineola** Fabr.

a. Black stripe of prothorax wider, angulated at the sides; *angulatus* Say.

3.—Legs black, piceous or testaceous..4.

    Legs bright yellow...5.

4.—Entirely black, side margin of prothorax very narrow about the middle.
Very similar to *fraxini*, but differs in the form of the claws and in the
prothoracic margin; it is the analogue of the European *atra* Linn. Length
5 mm.; Il. B. Terr.; Anticosti............................9. **nigritulus** n. sp.

    Prothorax yellow, with a broad dorsal black stripe, side margin rather strongly
reflexed; legs piceous or testaceous. Length 4.5—6 mm.; Can.; Ill.; Fla.
Penn.; L. Sup...10. **rectus** Mels.

    a.—Prothorax yellow, without dorsal stripe.

    β.—Elytra with entire margin pale.

    Black, only the sides of the prothorax yellow; prothorax wider than long,
disc not excavated each side near the margin, sides nearly uniformly rather
strongly margined; elytra more coarsely and sparsely rugose; claws with
a strong acute tooth; antennæ half as long as the body; ♀. Length
3 mm.; Detroit... 11. **manulus** n. sp.

5.—Piceous, mouth, prothorax, margins of elytra and legs yellow; antennæ long
and slender...6.

    Antennæ stouter; prothorax with a black cloud, wider than long, disc very
feebly excavated each side in front of the middle; side margin nearly
uniform in width; tibiæ and tarsi dusky. Length 6.5 mm.: Ga.: one
specimen...12. **cruralis** Lec.

    Black, mouth, base of antennæ, legs and prothorax orange-yellow, the latter
with a black dorsal line, wider than long, disc broadly concave each side in
front of the middle, side margin strongly reflexed, nearly uniform in width;
antennæ rather stout, but little shorter than the body, second joint one-third
as long as the third. ♀ antennæ two-thirds as long as the body, second
joint nearly half as long as the third. Length 6 mm.: Ill.; Ks.

13. flavipes Lec.

    a.—Prothorax entirely orange-yellow; *dichrous* Lec.; perhaps a distinct
species: Ks.; Tex.

6.—Prothorax wider than long, disc broadly concave each side in front of the
middle, side margin of nearly uniform width, strongly reflexed; disc with
or without a piceous cloud. Length 3.5—7 mm.; Atlantic region.

14. scitulus Say.

    a.—Pale yellow above, elytral stripe wanting. *nigriceps* Lec.

    Prothorax not wider than long, disc more strongly concave each side before
the middle, sides subsinuate, margin strongly reflexed, narrower for a short
distance behind the middle; elytra with pale margin narrower. The type
specimens of this species are pale yellow, but the form of the prothorax
sufficiently distinguishes it from *scitulus* and is quite characteristic. Length
4—6 mm.; Va.; Ga.... ... .15. **pusillus** Lec.

    More robust, prothorax entirely yellow, one-half wider than long, sides
rounded, margin reflexed, of nearly uniform width; (approaches in form
a ♀ *Silis*); antennæ piceous, base testaceous. Length 5 mm.: Ks.: Ill.;
Mich.; Ga.......................... .... 16. **luteicollis** Germ.

7.—Black: prothorax reddish-yellow, longer than wide, scarcely narrowed from
the base to the tip, sides subsinuate, margin reflexed, narrow; antennæ
long, slender, but little shorter than the body, entirely black, second joint

one-half as long as the third; claws slender, more acutely cleft than usual. Length 6 mm.; Col., La Veta: (Schwarz); one ♂.....17. **ruficollis** n. sp.

Yellow, antennæ (except base of first joint), elytral vitta, apical part of thighs, tibiæ and tarsi black; prothorax longer than wide, slightly narrowed in front, sides subsinuate, margin narrower behind the middle: antennæ two-thirds as long as the body, second joint one-half as long as the third. Length 7 mm.: Fla.; Ga..18. **longulus** Lec. This species resembles in appearance some of the varieties of *pusillus*, but is easily recognized by the longer prothorax.

a.—Pale yellow, antennæ (except at base), and tarsi dusky.

C.

This division is represented in our fauna by but a single species not unlike *flavipes* in appearance, but differing by the antennæ and legs being entirely black, and by the form of the claws. Those of the front pair are cleft or acutely toothed, while those of the middle and hind legs are squarely appendiculate. Otherwise there is nothing remarkable about the species.

Black, antennæ about one-half as long as the body, a little longer in ♂, second joint one-half as long as third, entirely black. Prothorax yellow, sometimes with a narrow black dorsal line, wider than long, sides straight, sides nearly uniformly-margined. Elytra rather densely granulato-rugose. Length 4.5 mm.: Texas; (Belfrage)...19. **impar** n. sp.

D.

These species occur on both sides of the continent, and among them are the largest in our fauna.

Eyes large and prominent, prothorax not or but little wider than long, fourth tarsal joint deeply bilobed, broadly and deeply concave each side in front of the middle, margin very narrow near the base; elytra finely granulato-rugose, and sparsely punctured and subtuberculate..........................2.

Eyes smaller, not prominent, prothorax transverse, sides more broadly margined..3.

2.—Prothorax slightly wider than long (♀) or longer than wide (♂): yellow-brown, head and prothorax more yellow, antennæ piceous, yellow at base; knees, tibiæ and tarsi piceous; ventral segments sometimes dusky: ♂ with the inner angle of hind tibiæ not produced. Length 12—19 mm.; Cal., S. Diego, Kern Co..20. **corsors** Lec.

Similar to the preceding but smaller, prothorax ♀ not wider than long; yellow, elytra and ventral segments often piceous, epipleuræ yellow; ♂ with inner angle of hind tibiæ spiniform. Length 12—14 mm.: L. S.; N. H.; Va.; Ill...21. **rotundicollis** Say.

Very similar to *rotundicollis*, but the elytra are uniform grayish-piceous, epipleuræ not yellow; ventral segments piceous, last one yellow; legs tinged with dusky: ♂ with tip of hind tibiæ not produced. Length 10 mm.; H. B. Terr.: L. Sup.; B. Col...................................22. **Curtisii** Kirby.

3. -Ventral segments ferruginous..4.

Ventral segments black, sides and apex yellow ....5.

Ventral segments black...6.

4. -Head and prothorax entirely yellow; antennæ with two basal joints yellow. Length 9 mm.; Cal.. ....23. **transmarinus** Motsch.
Head and prothorax yellow, the former black behind the eyes: antennæ with two basal joints yellow. Length 8 mm.; Cal......24. **grandicollis** Lec.
Head black, with the mouth and front yellow; antennæ entirely black; prothorax yellow with a large black anterior spot. Length 8 mm.; N. Mex.; Col ....25. **fidelis** Lec.
a.—Head black, sides of front testaceous.

5.—Mouth and prothorax yellow; the latter with a black dorsal stripe wider at the front margin, abbreviated behind, not attaining the base; antennæ entirely black. Length 6—9 mm.; Or.; B. Col........26. **oregonus** Lec.
a.- Prothoracic black stripe reduced to a discoidal spot; *scopus* Lec.
β.—Prothorax entirely yellow, basal joints of antennæ yellow beneath; (♀).
This form resembles *grandicollis*, and differs chiefly by the ventral segments not being entirely ferruginous or yellow.

6.—Mouth and prothorax yellow, the latter with a broad black dorsal stripe; ♀ with the prothorax wider than in the ♂, and antennæ half as long as the body; ♂ antennæ two-thirds as long as the body, stouter, subserrate. Length 5—7 mm.; Can.; Pa.; Ky.; L. Sup.; *armiger* Couper
27. **impressus** Lec.
The individuals with wide prothoracic vitta, especially the ♂ ♂ resemble *lincola*, but are at once recognized by the form of the claws; it varies as follows:
a.—Prothoracic stripe narrow, wider along the basal and apical margins; *tuberculatus* Lec.
β.—Prothorax entirely yellow: *collaris* Lec.

7. -Black, prothorax moderately margined, yellow, with two large black spots, mouth testaceous. Length 7 mm.; Col., Garland; Wy., Como.
28. **alticola** n. sp.
Ferruginous, transverse band of head, two large prothoracic spots, knees, tibiæ, tarsi and elytra black, the latter with side margin yellow, metathorax dusky, antennæ black, first joint pale beneath; prothorax very widely margined, sparsely punctured. Length 6—7 mm.; Atlantic region; Ks.
29. **bilineatus** Say.
a. Head and first joint of antennæ ferruginous.

E.

Black, mouth testaceous; prothorax yellow, with two large discoidal black spots connected on the median line. Length 6—8 mm.; Cal...30. **divisus** Lec.
Ferruginous, head behind the eyes, large prothoracic spot and elytra blackish; trunk and ventral segments dusky. Length 6—7 mm.; Cal.
31. **notatus** Mann.
a.—Yellow, elytra and prothoracic spot dusky; *larvalis* Lec.
Black, head in front of the eyes, prothorax, sides and apex of abdomen yellow. Length 7—10 mm.; Cal..32. **lautus** Lec.
Similar to *lautus*, but legs also ferruginous. Length 9 mm.; Cal., San Diego; (Bolter)..33. **ochropus** n. sp.

F.

The basal dilatation of the claws is more distinct in ♂ than ♀, and both of the front claws seem to be cleft in that sex.

Black; head in front of the eyes dull reddish; palpi and antennæ black. Prothorax longer than wide, polished, shining, rufo-testaceous, disc broadly concave before the middle at the sides, side margin behind the middle not reflexed, posterior callosities rather prominent. Elytra with feeble elevated lines, rugosely punctured and sparsely tuberculate: claws slender, simple, anterior one of the middle and hind tarsi feebly dilated at base; ♂ ♀: ♂ front tarsi with first joint longer and broadly dilated. Length 9 mm.; Nev.............34. **ingenuus** n. sp.

G.

A single species represents this group in our fauna. It resembles in form *impressus*, but is easily recognized by the color, and by the claws.

Piceous black, front part of head testaceous, prothorax wider than long, side margin wide, disc pale, with a broad black dorsal stripe dilated before and behind the middle; there a large rounded elevation each side in the pale part in front of the middle, the posterior elevations are small, rather prominent, and situated in the black stripe; elytra finely scabrous, margin pale: antennæ longer in ♂ than ♀, piceous, testaceous at base: claws slender, not toothed nor cleft; ♂ ♀. Length 5 mm.; Ga.; Fla.; (Bolter)...............................35. **marginellus** Lec.

POLEMIUS Lec.

This genus is intermediate between *Telephorus* and *Silis*, and is sufficiently defined by the characters given in the table. The species are but few, and none have yet been observed in the Pacific region, nor have any been indicated from other districts.

Prothorax with front angles obtuse, but obvious.....................................2.
Prothorax with the apical margin rounded into the sides without angles; disc nearly flat, smooth, without impressions, side margin obliquely and feebly interrupted at the middle, inflexed flanks deeply transversely impressed; black, prothorax, and sometimes the humeri yellow; the former occasionally marked with a dusky dorsal line; antennæ feebly serrate, three-fourths as long as the body in ♂, somewhat shorter in ♀. Length 7—9 mm.; Tex.; N. Mex...1. **planicollis** Lec.
2.—Prothorax nicked in front of the middle, side margin very narrow near the tip ....3.
Prothorax transverse, widely margined, nicked about the middle.................4.
3.—Black, prothorax with a narrow fulvous margin, humeri often fulvous; disc of prothorax transversely impressed each side near the margin, which is narrowly reflexed and acutely interrupted in front of the middle; elytra densely scabrous with distinct elevated lines; ♂ antennæ long, strongly serrate: ♀ antennæ shorter, less serrate, prothorax wider and more strongly margined. Length 6—7 mm.; Pa.; Ill.; Fla.; Tex...2. **laticornis** Say.
a.—Prothorax rather narrower, elytra less coarsely scabrous: *incisus* Lec.
Very similar to *laticornis*, but the prothorax is pale tinged with rose, with a dorsal dark vitta wider behind; the sides are more broadly margined; elytra densely scabrous. Length 7 mm.; Pa.; Ga.; Tex.....3. **repandus** n. sp.
a.—Prothoracic vitta indistinct; elytra with margins pale ♀.
Type.— Prothorax wider with the sides subbisinuate; antennæ shorter.

4.—Black or piceous: prothorax transverse, not narrowed in front, side margin of
nearly uniform width, nicked about the middle; ferruginous or yellow, with
a black dorsal line: elytra densely scabrous, with pale margins. ♀ prothorax
bisinuate on the sides, antennæ shorter than in the ♂. Length 3.5—5 mm.;
Pa.; Fla.; Tex.. ....4. **limbatus** Lec.
a.—Prothorax without dorsal vitta.
β.—Elytral pale margin obsolete.

SILIS Charp.

The table of species given by me,* requires modification to permit
the introduction of several new species, which have since been collected.
To avoid the inconvenience of referring to the previous volume, I have
changed its form as follows : † the characters being taken from the ♂ ♂ .

Base of prothorax broadly rounded, not lobed, sides excavated into a deep
round cavity near the base; both angles of the excavation acute, ante-basal
appendage acute, spiniform...**A.**

Base of prothorax lobed, excavation of hind angles partly basal, angles therefore not very distinct though acute, anterior margin of excavation sinuate with
two prominent but rounded angles: ante-basal appendage acute, spiniform, directed
acutely backwards..**B.**

Base of prothorax lobed, deeply foveate inside of the hind angles which are
therefore more prominent and acute; incisure near the base moderately deep, with
the anterior angle rounded: ante-basal process compressed, rounded at tip.........**C.**

Base of prothorax not lobed, broadly reflexed; excavation entirely lateral,
anterior angle of incisure nearly rectangular, hind angle long, acute, produced
into a slender filament which is bent forwards . ...**D.**

Base of prothorax not lobed, posterior process of incisure not ante-basal, as in
the preceding groups of species, but proceeding from the base itself, by an exten-
sion of the hind angles; this process, as well as the anterior one is compressed
and obtuse at tip...**E.**

A.

Yellow testaceous, head, antennæ and legs more or less dusky; ♀ prothorax very
transverse, rounded on the sides which are feebly sinuate near the base,
much narrowed in front, ♂ ♀. Length 7 mm.; Or.....1. **spinigera** Lec.
Black, prothorax bright reddish yellow, formed as in *spinigera*, from which it
differs chiefly by color and more slender body: (perhaps the fully developed
form of that species). Length 7 mm.; Atlanta. Id., (Allgewahr): Garland,
Col., (Schwarz)............ ....2. **minuta** n. sp.

* Trans. Am. Ent. Soc. 1874, 60.
† It must be noticed that in this genus, as in several others in Coleoptera, the
specific characters are exhibited chiefly in the ♂; in not a small number of instances in such genera the ♀ ♀ of different species are as yet undistinguishable.
Some of the sexual characters in this genus seem to have escaped the attention of
European observers. The anterior claw of the front tarsi, namely, of the ♀ is
more or less toothed at base, and the inflexed flank of the prothorax at the first
quarter of its length with a fine transverse line, which runs to the side margin,
and represents the nick already mentioned as occurring in both sexes of *Polemius*.
The penultimate ventral segment is cleft to the base in the ♂, exposing the whole
length of the eighth segment.

B.

Basal excavations of prothorax moderate; color black, prothorax yellow. ♂ ♀.
Length 5 mm.; L. Sup.: H. B. Terr.: N. Mex............3. **difficilis** Lec.

Basal excavations of prothorax larger; prothorax and elytra pale yellow. ♂ ♀.
Length 6 mm.: Cal.; Nev............................... ....4. **flavida** Lec.

C.

Basal impressions of prothorax very deep, hind angles strongly carinated; upper
surface pale yellow...2.

Basal impressions of prothorax much smaller, hind angles feebly carinated; black,
prothorax more or less yellow........... ....3.

2.—Incisure of hind angles of prothorax deep, appendage straight. Length
5 mm: Or........................... ....5. **cava** Lec.
Incisure of hind angles broad, appendage curved. Length 6 mm.
6. **pallida** Mann.

3.— Incisure of hind angles deep, appendage long. Length 5 mm.: Can.; Mich.
7. **percomis** Say.
Incisure of hind angles shallow, appendage short. Length 6 mm.: Or.
8. **vulnerata** Lec.

D.

Elytra and prothorax pale, the latter sometimes with a black dorsal vitta. Length
5—6 mm.: Cal.................................... ....9. **lutea** Lec.

Black, prothorax yellow, sometimes with a black dorsal vitta. Length 3.6 mm.:
Cal.......... ....10. **filigera** Lec.

E.

Prothorax strongly margined, but not lobed at base; both processes narrow,
parallel, directed outwards; black, prothorax reddish-yellow, basal margin
blackish. Length 4.5 mm.; Ill. ....11. **spathulata** n. sp.

♂ antennae nearly as long as the body, joints 3—10 about four times longer
than wide, slightly broader at tip, therefore subserrate.

♀ antennae one-half as long as the body, not serrate.

Prothorax broadly truncate at the middle of the base, then sinuate near the
angles, which are produced into a large triangular plate; the posterior
margin of this plate is directed outwards, and the anterior margin outwards
and backwards; the anterior process of the incisure is directed obliquely
outwards and backwards; it is truncate at tip, and overlaps the basal
process, so as to produce the appearance of a perforation; color ferruginous
yellow, antennae, palpi, legs and elytra black, the last with pruinose pubescence; head black, front reddish. Length 6 mm.: Texas, (Belfrage).
12. **perforata** n. sp.

♂ antennae three-fourths as long as the body, scarcely subserrate.

♀ unknown.

DITEMNUS Lec.

This genus differs from *Silis* chiefly by the much wider antennae, and
the sides of prothorax lobed in such manner as to present two incisures;
one near the tip formed by the thickened apical margin, the other near
the base, between the two processes, which are obtuse, compressed and
directed outwards. Besides this the base is (in the typical species *bidentatus*), acutely nicked at the inner end of the posterior or basal process;

the base is strongly margined and the disc deeply excavated.   In the ♂ the antennæ are longer and serrate; the seventh ventral is cleft to the base, with the eighth narrow and visible for its whole length.   The Brazilian *Pachymesia* Westw., seems to be allied to this genus.

Black, pruinose with gray pubescence, prothorax yellow, apical lobe of sides well defined, prominent, middle lobe narrow, prominent horizontally, hind lobe straight, equally prominent. Length 3.5 mm.; Pa.: Ga.....1. **bidentatus** Say.

Black, prothorax red, anterior margin much less reflexed, and apical side lobe therefore indistinct; middle lobe wide, with its posterior margin straight, and anterior margin convexly curved, hind lobe bent slightly forwards; disc deeply and widely excavated. Length 5 mm.; Cala....................2. : **blusus** Lec.

Black, pubescent with gray hair, prothorax and side margin of elytra yellow, the former with a very deep discoidal fossa, the apical side lobe indistinct, middle one broad, prominent, with the anterior margin convexly curved, posterior margin straight; hind lobe long, compressed, well separated from the base, emarginate at tip and unguiculate: base truncate, very strongly margined; ♂. Length 4 5 mm.; Tex.; Ariz.; Dr. Horn..3. **fossiger** n. sp.

Group 3.—*Malthini.*

The species of this group are of small size and weak structure, remarkable chiefly for the short elytra, which leaves the wings partly exposed and folded along the dorsal surface of the abdomen.   I have modified the group as exposed by me in Classification Col. N. Am., by removing *Tytthonyx* which seems to have no relation to the other genera and to resemble them superficially merely by the abbreviated elytra.

The wealth of variation in sexual characters is greater in this group than in almost any other in Coleoptera.   In *Ichthyurus* it affects the middle legs of the ♂ , and in *Malthodes* the last abdominal segments of both sexes, and the forms of the claspers are quite as complex as those represented by Baron R. Osten Sacken in the Tipulidæ, with short palpi. Proc. Acad. Nat. Sc. Phila. 1859, pl. 3 & 4.   The species are probably numerous but have not yet received much attention from collectors.   The European species, which run somewhat parallel with ours, have been excellently illustrated by the late Dr. H. von Kiesenwetter, Linn. Ent. vii, pl. 2.

Palpi with the last joint elongate, securiform: metathoracic episterna wide in front, strongly triangular.........................   ....2.
Palpi with the last joint oval pointed: metathoracic episterna narrow; claws simple................   ....3.
2.—Claws appendiculate; mandibles toothed.. .   ...**TRYPHERUS** Lec.
   Claws simple...   ....**LOBETUS** Kw.
3.—Mandibles toothed, head wide, narrowed behind..............**MALTHINUS** Latr.
   Mandibles simple, head not narrowed behind......... ....**MALTHODES** Kw.

TRYPHERUS Lec.

By the kindness of Prof. Westwood, who presented me with a specimen of his very singular *Ichthyurus discoidalis*, I have been enabled to make a satisfactory comparison between it and *Trypherus* Lec. (*Lygerus* Kiesenw.), which is somewhat unfavorable to the retention of the latter as a distinct genus, though in the present condition of nomenclature it cannot be properly suppressed. The enormous inflation of the middle thighs of the ♂ in *I. discoidalis*, the extremely prolonged spiniform trochanters, and the very short tibiæ of the same pair of legs would lead one on superficial inspection to regard the two insects as distinct generic types. But I find that in the ♂ of *T. latipennis* the middle trochanters are larger than in the ♀, pointed at the end and angulated or even toothed near the base; the middle thighs are also decidedly thicker than in the ♀, though there is no difference in the tibiæ. The last abdominal segments are similarly modified in the two species, though much more strongly so in the Oriental than in the American species. In the former the last dorsal is emarginate or bilobed, and is moreover deeply excavated beneath; the seventh ventral is truncate behind, and the eighth narrower and much smaller. In *T. latipennis* the last dorsal is only broadly emarginate, and there is a small anal segment; the seventh ventral is deeply emarginate, the eighth is more complex in arrangement with some small processes, which are difficult to describe, and as there is but one species, quite unimportant for the recognition of the same. The eyes in both genera are large and prominent in the ♂.

Piceous, more or less varied with testaceous, elytra nearly twice as long as the prothorax, rugosely punctured, tips rounded, testaceous; antennæ one-half as long as the body, slender, dusky, testaceous at base, third joint equal to the second, a little shorter than the fourth; ♀ with last dorsal segment trilobed at tip; last ventral oblique and subsinuate each side, prolonged at the middle. Length 7 mm.; Pa.; Va.; Ga............ ....**latipennis** Germ.

LOBETUS Kiesenw.

The species referred by me to this genus differs from the South American *torticollis* in having the ♂ antennæ in no respect distorted or different from those of the ♀, but this is a character of merely specific value. The hind legs of the ♂ are longer than in the ♀, slender, the thighs and tibiæ somewhat curved. The penultimate ventral segment in the ♂ is broadly emarginate, and the last one is oval, large and convex, very much as in *Chauliognathus*. The antennæ are inserted between and near to the eyes, which are moderate in both sexes.

Black, prothorax, tip of elytra and abdomen (except the last two dorsal and ventral segments), ferruginous; ♀ penultimate dorsal segment broadly emarginate, last one small, triangular, obtusely rounded; penultimate ventral nicked at tip, last one small, exposed. Length 2.5—4 mm.: Ga.: Fla.: Tex.
                                                                    abdominalis Lec.

MALTHINUS Latr.

The head is large in this genus, narrowed behind the eyes as in *Podabrus*, which it obviously represents in this group; the antennæ slender, with the second joint not shorter than the following ones, somewhat distant from the eyes, which are lateral and moderately prominent. Last joint of palpi oval, acutely pointed at tip. Elytra three-fourths as long as the abdomen, punctured in rows in our species. Last dorsal segment of ♂ not lobed but rounded; penultimate ventral emarginate, last ventral oval, large and convex, as in *Chauliognathus;* ♀ with last ventral emarginate at tip.

Piceous, prothorax smooth and scutel ferruginous, elytra entirely black, anterior half of head, base of antennæ and front legs yellow. Length 3 mm.; Tex.: (Belfrage)...1. **atripennis** n. sp.

Piceous or testaceous, prothorax punctured, sides of prothorax and tip of elytra yellow. Length 3 mm.; Va.; Ga..2. **occipitalis** Lec.

The paler specimens are *difficilis* Lec.; this species is very closely allied to, and perhaps not different from the European *fasciatus*.

MALTHODES Kiesenw.

As above mentioned, the insects of this genus have not been very thoroughly collected, and from the meagre contents of the collections of Dr. Horn and myself, not exceeding ninety examples, I have constructed the following table of the species which seem to be indicated in our fauna. The characters are derived from the ♂ ♂ .

Last abdominal segments normal in both sexes..**A.**
Last abdominal segments ♂ inflated and variously modified ....**B.**
Last abdominal segments ♂ with long complex processes..........................**C.**

A.

Piceous tinged with testaceous, prothorax nearly twice as wide as long, sides finely margined, more strongly so near and at the sides of the base; elytra two-thirds the length of the wings; ♂ head wider than prothorax, eyes small, prominent, antennæ extending behind the elytra, as long as the wings, second joint equal to third, penultimate ventral segment emarginate, last segment triangular, rounded at tip. Length 2—3 mm.; Pa.; Ga................. 1. **spado** Lec.

B.

Piceous head blackish; prothorax twice as wide as long, sides parallel and strongly margined, subsinuate and wider at the front angles which are rounded; elytra three-fourths as long as the wings; ♂ head wider than the prothorax, eyes moderately large, prominent, antennæ extending to tip of elytra, second joint equal to third, penultimate ventral segment large and more convex, emarginate, last segment prominent, obtusely rounded at tip, accessory processes short, neither slender nor prominent. Length 3 mm.; Cal.....................2. **laticollis** Lec.

Of the same color as the preceding, antennæ and abdomen sometimes partly testaceous; prothorax one-half wider than long, sides narrowly margined, concavely transversely impressed near the front angles which are rounded; elytra two-thirds as long as the wings; ♂ head wider than prothorax, eyes very large, convex, prominent, antennæ rather stout, extending behind the elytra, as long as the wings, second joint equal to third: penultimate ventral segment convex, inflated, larger in fact than the head, embracing the penultimate dorsal on the sides, emarginate behind, and deeply and broadly excavated; lateral lobes broad, large, triangular; last ventral elongate, broad at base, then produced as a narrow obliquely ascending process slightly nicked at tip; penultimate dorsal large, last dorsal transverse, broadly emarginate, fringed behind, concave beneath: accessory processes not seen. Length 2—3 mm.; N. H.; Mass.; Pa.......................3. **concavus** Lec.

C.

Last dorsal segments not prolonged.. 2.
Last dorsal segments prolonged...5.
2.—Last ventral segment narrow, prolonged, cleft or nicked at tip ....3.
    Last ventral segment wider, parallel............................ ....4.
    Last ventral slender forked, slender, piceous, base of antennæ, narrow head of prothorax and base of antennæ testaceous; prothorax smooth, a little wider than long, very narrowly margined, anterior and posterior angles impressed; antennæ ♂ nearly as long. ♀ about one-half as long as the body, second joint two-thirds as long as third ; ♂ last dorsal segment obtusely rounded without processes, seventh ventral prolonged into a very slender process, which is strongly curved, and deeply forked with diverging processes at the tip. Length 3 mm.; Va.; Deer Park............11. **captiosus** n. sp.
3.—Last ventral ♂ straight, margined each side, narrower towards the tip, which is acutely nicked. Piceous, prothorax tinged with testaceous, transverse, finely margined, front angles obliquely truncate; antennæ ♂ two-thirds, ♀ one-half as long as the body, with fourth and following joints longer than the second or third. Length 2—3 mm.; Pa.; Va.; Ga.; Cal.
                                                    4. **fragilis** Lec.
    Very similar to *fragilis* but the prothorax, front legs, and base of the antennæ are yellow, ♂ last ventral is narrower, prolonged, channeled, and acutely emarginate at tip. Length 2.5—3 mm.; Pa.; Md............5. **exilis** Mels.
    Last ventral ♂ bent in a sinuate manner obliquely upwards, and more deeply nicked at tip than in *fragilis*, prothorax transverse, finely margined, tinged with testaceous; head black, eyes large, prominent, antennæ long, slender, fourth and following joints longer than second or third, ♂ two-thirds, ♀ one-half as long as the body. Length 3 mm.; Cal............6. **fusculus** Lec.
    a.—Prothorax yellow testaceous. ♀.
    Last ventral ♂ stouter, straight, scarcely nicked at tip; testaceous, head black, eyes moderately large, prothorax transverse, finely margined, elytra piceous at tip; antennæ stout, piceous, with first and second joints testaceous, third joint not shorter than fourth, in ♂ nearly as long, in ♀ about two-thirds as long as the body. Length 2—3 mm.; Va.; Ga................7. **rectus** n. sp.
4.—Last ventral ♂ large, parallel, curved upwards, channeled for its whole length, deeply emarginate or rather forked at tip; last dorsal with two short acute processes; accessory processes slender but small; piceous, head black, prothorax rufo-piceous, legs testaceous, the former a little wider than long, side margin very narrow, front angles impressed; antennæ rather stout, as long as the elytra, third joint not shorter than fourth (♂). Length 3 mm.; Ill.; one ♂......... ....8. **curvatus** n. sp.
    Similar to *curvatus*, but the last ventral is testaceous and narrower, with the fork more slender, penultimate ventral deeply emarginate; penultimate

dorsal with lateral deflexed processes; black, eyes large, antennæ as long as elytra, third joint scarcely shorter than fourth; prothorax strongly margined and transversely impressed.   Length 2—3 mm.; Col., Veta Pass.

                                                                        9. **furcifer** n. sp.

5.—Last dorsal prolonged, received in the fork of the greatly prolonged last
   ventral..6.

Last dorsal with two long slender processes, receiving between them the elongate last ventral; the latter curved upwards in the arc of a circle, not cleft at the tip, but obliquely flattened (or beveled) on the under side, and pubescent: accessory processes slender, long, spiniform, directed obliquely downwards and backwards, nearer the median line are two other stout processes directed backwards and between them a small furcate object, which is perhaps the intramittent organ.   Length 3 mm.; Md.; one pair, (Zimmermann)........ ....10. **arcifer** n. sp.

6.—Last ventral ♂ large, broadly channeled, curved upwards in the arc of a circle, furcate at tip, receiving in the fork the last dorsal which is narrow and nicked at tip; accessory processes not developed; penultimate dorsal normal in form.   Piceous, head blackish, eyes large, antennæ longer than elytra, first joint testaceous, third scarcely shorter than fourth; prothorax one-half wider than long, narrowly margined, tinged with testaceous.   Length 2.5— 3.5 mm.; L. Superior, and N. II...............12. **fuliginosus** Lec.

Last ventral testaceous, immensely long, narrow, bent sigmoidly upwards, dilated into a broad and large deflexed terminal fork, which receives the narrow deflexed last dorsal; penultimate ventral broadly emarginate; penultimate dorsal greatly elongated, concave beneath, with a large lateral deflexed marginal tooth near the hinder end.   Black, eyes moderately large, antennæ stout, as long as the elytra, third joint a little longer than second, shorter than fourth; prothorax twice as wide as long, strongly margined. Length 3 mm.; L. Super.; N. II., Mt. Washington...........13. **niger** Lec.

Unclassified females.*

Head black, convex, densely punctulate, eyes small; antennæ slender, extending to end of elytra piceous, joints 2—4 nearly equal, first joint yellow.   Prothorax bright yellow, not wider than long, transversely convex, sides narrowly margined, front angles obliquely truncate.   Scutel and elytra piceous, finely rugosely punctured as usual, half as long as the abdomen; abdomen yellow with last two dorsal and ventral segments black; metasternum dusky, legs yellow, partly dusky. Length 4 mm.; Middle States; one ♀..............................14. **analis** n. sp.

Dusky, prothorax fusco-testaceous, one-half wider than long, sides parallel, strongly margined; head densely punctulate, darker piceous, occiput feebly channeled, eyes small, antennæ stout reaching to the middle of the elytra, joints 2—4 nearly equal.   Elytra nearly as long as the abdomen, three-fourths as long as the wings, finely rugosely punctured.   Differs from *fragilis* by sides of prothorax straighter and angles better defined.   Length 2.5 mm.; Va.; one ♀.

                                                                  15. **congruus** n. sp.

_____

* The specimens mentioned under this head cannot be properly apportioned to the ♂ ♂ which are tabulated.   Therefore when any ♀ forms are collected, which do not find their place as above stated, it will be prudent for the collector to ascertain if they may not with some probability be referred to the species indicated under this head.

Dusky, head blackish, larger, wider than prothorax, densely punctulate, eyes larger and more prominent; prothorax not wider than long, dull yellow, sides parallel, strongly margined, broadly impressed near the front angles, antennæ rather stout, extending beyond the middle of the elytra, first joint testaceous, 2—4 nearly equal. Elytra two-thirds as long as the wings, rugosely punctured. Differs from *fragilis* and *exilis* by prothorax not wider than long. Length 2.5 mm.; Lake Superior; one ♀ ....16. **quadricollis** n. sp.

Much smaller, pale inclining to dusky; head piceous, not wider than prothorax, punctulate, eyes moderately large, antennæ stout, extending to middle of elytra, black or piceous, first joint pale, second joint a trifle longer than third, outer joints not much longer than wide. Prothorax wider than long, sides strongly margined, front angles obliquely truncate, more reflexed and prominent than usual. Elytra two-thirds as long as the wings, rugosely punctured. Length 1 mm.; L. Super. and Mass..17. **parvulus** Lec.

Bibliography and Synonymy.

Sub-family I.—*Lycidæ*.

LYCUS Fabr.

1. **L. cruentus** Lec., Proc. Acad. Nat. Sc. Phila. 1861, 336.[*]

LYCOSTOMUS Motsch.

1. **L. lateralis** Mels., (*Lycus*), Proc. Acad. Nat. Sc. Phila. ii, 302; Lec. Journ. Acad. Nat. Sc. Phila. 2d. ser. i, 73.
2. **L. fulvellus** n. sp. ante, 18.

RHYNCHEROS Lec. n. g.

1. **R. sanguinipennis** Say, (*Lycus*), Journ. Acad. Nat. Sc. Phila. iii, 178; ed. Lec. ii, 116; Say, Am. Ent. ii, pl. 21; ed. Lec. i, 45.

CALOPTERON Guér.

1. **C. megalopteron** Lec., Proc. Acad. Nat. Sc. Phila. 1861, 349.
2. **C. terminale** Say, (*Lycus*), Journ. Acad. Nat. Sc. Phila. iii, 178; ed. Lec. ii, 116; Say, Am. Ent. ii, pl. 21; ed. Lec. i, 44; Lec. loc. cit. i, 75; [Var.] *Digr. divisa* Newm. Ent. Mag. v, 381; Waterh. Types, i, 22, pl. vi. f. 2: form typ. *reticulatum* ‡ Lec. (nec Fabr.) loc. cit. i, 75; *Digr. dorsalis* Newm. Ent. Mag. v, 386; Waterh. loc. cit. i, 22, pl. vi, f. 3; *duplicatum* Hald. Proc. Acad. Nat. Sc. Phila. i, 203.
3. **C. reticulatum** Fabr., (*Lycus*), Syst. Ent. 203; Syst. El. ii, 111; Oliv. Ins. 29, 7, pl. 1, f. 7; Anon. Biol. Centr. Am. Lycidæ, pl. 1, 17; *Digr. typica* Newm. Ent. Mag. v, 380; Lec. loc. cit. i, 21, pl. vi, f. 1; *Digr. discrepans* Newm. Ent. Mag. v, 381; var. *Digr. affinis* Lec. loc. cit. i, 75; var. *Digr. apicalis* Lec. ibid. 75.†

---

[*] **L. cruentus** Fabr., Syst. El. 114, from Sumatra is an older homonym of this species, but as it seems to be dropped out of modern bibliography, I do not think it necessary to change at present the name of the species described by me.

† In the table on p. 20 (above) the name *reticulatum* should be changed to *terminale*, and *typicum* to *reticulatum* to correspond with synonymy here given,

4. **C. retiferum** n. sp. ante, 20.
5. **C. tricarinatum** n. sp. ante, 20, 21.

CÆNIA Newm.

1. **C. dimidiata** Fabr., (*Lycus*), Syst. El. ii, 111; Lec. loc. cit. 76; var. *scapularis* Newm. Ent. Mag. v, 381 : Waterh. loc. cit. i, 23, pl. vi, f. 6.
2. **C. amplicornis** n. sp. ante. 22.

CELETES Newm.

1. **C. basalis** Lec., loc. cit. 76; Waterh. loc. cit. 23, pl. vi, f. 4; *marginella* ‡ Newm. Ent. Mag. v, 381 : var. *mystacina* Lec. loc. cit. 77; var. *tabida* Lec. ibid. 77.

LOPHEROS Lec. n. g.

1. **L. fraternus** Randall, (*Omalisus*), Bost. Journ. Nat. Hist. ii, 15.

EROS Newm.

1. **E. thoracicus** Randall, (*Omalisus*), Bost. Journ. Nat. Hist. ii, 14; *præfectus* Newm. Ent. Mag. v, 382; Waterh. loc. cit. i, 37, pl. ix, f. 6.
2. **E. hamatus** Mann., (*Dictyopterus*), Bull. Mosc. 1843, ii, 245.
3. **E. simplicipes** Mann., (*Dictyopt.*), Bull. Mosc. 1843, ii, 245.
4. **E. lætus** Motsch., (*Dictyoptera*), Schrenck, Amur, 115.
5. **E. coccinatus** Say, (*Omalisus*), Bost. Journ. Nat. Hist. i, 155; ed. Lec. ii, 633.
6. **E. mundus** Say, (*Omalisus*), ibid. i, 155; ed. Lec. ii, 633.
7. **E. sculptilis** Say, (*Omalisus*), ibid. i, 156; ed. Lec. ii, 633; Lec. Journ. Acad. Nat. Sc. Phila. 2d. i, 78; *axillaris* Mels. Proc. ejusd. ii, 302; *oblitus* Newm. Ent. Mag. v, 382 : *Erotides obl.* Waterh. loc. cit. i, 38, pl. ix, f. 9.
8. **E. humeralis** Fabr., (*Lycus*), Syst. El. ii, 111; Lec. loc. cit. i, 78, (syn. excl.); *Omal. obliquus* Say, Bost. Journ. Nat. Hist. i, 156; ed. Lec. ii, 634: *incestus* Lec. loc. cit. i, 78; *oblitus* ‡ Lec. ibid. (nec Newm.)
9. **E. trilineatus** Mels., Proc. Acad. Nat. Sc. Phila. ii, 303; Lec. loc. cit. i, 79.
10. **E. crenatus** Germ., (*Omal.*), Ins. Nov. 61; Lap. Hist. Nat. Col. i, 263; Lec. loc. cit. i, 79; *Omal. cruciatus* Randall, Bost. Journ. Nat. Hist. ii, 15.

PLATEROS Bourgeois.

1. **P. timidus** Lec., (*Eros*), loc. cit. i, 80.
2. **P. modestus** Say, (*Lycus*), Bost. Journ. Nat. Hist. i, 153; ed. Lec. ii, 631.
3. **P. canaliculatus** Say, (*Lycus*), ibid. i, 154; ed. Lec. ii, 632; *alatus* Newm. Ent. Mag. v, 382; Waterh. loc. cit. i, 26, pl. viii, f. 4; *Eros socius* Lec. loc. cit. i, 81.
4. **P. sollicitus** Lec., (*Eros*), Journ. Acad. Nat. Sc. Phila. 2d. i, 83; *lascivus* Lec. ibid. i, 83.
5. **P. lictor** Newm., (*Eros*), Ent. Mag. v, 382 : Waterh. loc. cit. i, 25, pl. viii, f. 5 : *nanus* Mels. (*Dict.*), Proc. Ac. Nat. Sc. Phila. ii, 302; *mollis* Lec. loc. cit. 83 : *vilis* Lec. ibid. 83.
6. **P. floralis** Mels., (*Dictyopterus*), Proc. Acad. Nat. Sc. Phila. ii, 302; *minutus* Lec. loc. cit. 82.

Lycus marginellus Fabr., Syst. El. ii, 118, evidently belongs to this genus, but is irrecognizable, and should be dropped from the lists.

which is the best I can give for the variable species in our fauna. Their true relations can only be ascertained by a more profound and careful study of the tropical species with which they are allied, and which seem to have been multiplied in the books without measure and without distinctive characters.

LYGISTOPTERUS Muls.

1. **L. rubripennis** Lec., (*Dictyoptera*), Trans. Amer. Ent. Soc. 1875, 172.

CALOCHROMUS Guér.

1. **C. fervens** n. sp. ante, 28.
2. **C. perfacetus** Say, (*Lycus*), Am. Ent. pl. 21; ed. Lec. i, 46; *Dictyopterus substriatus* Lec. Journ. Acad. Nat. Sc. Phila. 2d, i, 74.
3. **C. ruficollis** Lec., (*Dictyoptera*), Trans. Amer. Ent. Soc. 1875, 172.
4. **C. dimidiatus** Lec., (*Dict.*), ibid. 172.

Sub-family II.—*Lampyridæ*.

Tribe 1.—*Lampyrini*.

MATHETEUS Lec.

1. **M. Theveneti** Lec., Trans. Amer. Ent. Soc. Phila. 1874, 58.

POLYCLASIS Newm.

1. **P. bifaria** Say, (*Lampyris*), Bost. Journ. Nat. Hist. i. 137; ed. Lec. Proc. Acad. Nat. Sc. Phila. ii, 332; *ovata* Newm. Ent. Mag. v, 383.

LUCIDOTA Lap.*

1. **L. atra** Fabr., Ent. Syst. i. 2, 101, (*Lamp.*); Oliv. Ent. 28, 27, pl. 3, f. 28; Enc. Méth. Lec. loc. cit. 332; *laticornis* Fabr. ibid. i, 2, 99; Syst. El. ii, 100; Lap. Hist. Nat. i, 268, (*Photinus*); Motsch. Et. Ent. 1853, 4, (*Lychnuris?*); *Lychnuris morio* Mels. Proc. Acad. Nat. Sc. Phila. ii, 203; var. *tarda* Lec. loc. cit. 332.
2. **L. punctata** Lec. loc. cit. 333.

ELLYCHNIA Lec.

1. **E. flavicollis** Lec., (*Photinus*), Trans. Am. Ent. Soc. 1868, 53.
2. **E. californica** Motsch., Et. Ent. 1853, 3.

---

* This generic name should probably be rejected for the species here mentioned; it was proposed (Ann. Soc. Ent. Fr. 1st, ii, 136), for species with ramose antennæ; the universally known and common species, *atra* Fabr., is not mentioned among them, and is referred to by Laporte under *Lucernuta*, the second division of *Photinus*, as No. 25, *P. laticornis*, ibid. 144. It is quite evident that the superficially observed characters used by him, like those of Motschulsky, can have no significance in a system like that which I have here attempted to introduce, for the very next species of *Photinus* (*Lucernuta*), is described as having a "luminous spot at the middle of the fourth ventral segment." This position of the lightorgan, barring the error in the numbering of the segments would place at least that species of *Lucernuta* in the neighborhood of *Pyractomena*. In the confusion of nomenclature thus produced it would perhaps be easier to retain for our species, and for as many from tropical America as are found to be congeneric with them, the Dejeanian name *Lychnuris*, first defined by me in Proc. Acad. Nat. Sc. Phila. ii, 332. Since, however, I am neither a "purist," nor "resurrectionist," but an humble conveyor of thought, endeavoring only to state distinctly the relations of the objects of which I have occasion to write, I leave this and many similar questions for those whose tastes lead them in another direction.

3. **E. corrusca** Linn., Syst. Nat. ed. xii, ii, 644;* *(Lamp.)*, Oliv. Ent. 28, 19, pl. 2,
f. 14; Fabr. Spec. Ent. i, 251; Syst. El. ii. 100; *latipennis* Motsch. Et.
Ent. 1853, 3; var. *autumnalis* Mels. Proc. Acad. Nat. Sc. Phila. ii, 303;
corrusca ‡ Motsch. Et. Ent. 1853, 2; var. *lacustris* Lec. loc. cit. 334.

PYROPYGA Motsch.

1. **P. luteicollis** Lec., *(Lucidota)*, Proc. Am. Phil. Soc. 1878, 405. (In the remarks
under this species *Ellychnia flavicollis* by an unfortunate clerical error is
mentioned as *collaris*).
2. **P. fenestralis** Mels., *(Pyractomena)*, Proc. Acad. Nat. Sc. Phila. ii, 304; Lec.
ibid. 1851, 218, (synon. emend.): *californica* Motsch. Et. Ent. 1853, 5;
Lucidota cal. Gorham, Trans. Ent. Soc. Lond. 1880, 17; *Ph. sobrinus*
Gorh. Biol. Cent. Am. 49; *Ph. reversus* Gemm. Ent. Hefte vi, 1870, 120,
(nomen superf.).
3. **P. nigricans** Say, *(Lamp.)*, Journ. Acad. Nat. Sc. Phila. iii, 179; ed. Lec. ii, 116;
Ellychnia nigr. Lec. Proc. loc. cit. ii, 333; Motsch. Et. Ent. 1853, 4.
4. **P. decipiens** Harris, Trans. Hartford Soc. 1836, 74, pl. 1, f. 2; Lec. loc. cit. ii,
333; *neglecta* ↓ Dej. Cat.
5. **P. minuta** Lec., loc. cit. ii. 333.
6. **P. indicta** n. sp. ante, 32.

TENASPIS Lec. n. g.

1. **T. angularis** Gorham, *(Hyas)*, Trans. Ent. Soc. Lond. 1880, 7, pl. 1, f. 19.

PYRACTOMENA Lec.

1. **P. angulata** Say. *(Lamp.)*, Journ. Acad. Nat. Sc. Phila. v, 162; ed. Lec. ii, 273;
Lec. loc. cit. 336, (syn. excl.); *(Pyractomena)*. Motsch. Et. Ent. 1853, 38.
2. **P. borealis** Randall, *(Lamp.)*, Bost. Journ. Nat. Hist. ii, 16; Lec. loc. cit. 336.
3. **P. ecostata** Lec., *(Photinus)*, Proc. Am. Phil. Soc. 1878, 406; *nitidiventris* Lec.
ibid. 406.
4. **P. lucifera** Mels., *(Lamp.)*, Proc. Acad. Nat. Sc. Phila. ii, 304; *linearis* Lec. loc.
cit. v, 336; *angustata* Lec. ibid. v, 336; *punctiventris* Lec. Proc. Am. Phil.
Soc. 1878, 407.

PHOTINUS Lap.

1. **P. consanguineus** Lec., loc. cit. 335: *vittiger* ‖ Lec. ibid. 336: *zonatus* Gemm.
Col. Hefte, vi, 1870, 120, (nomen superfluum).
2. **P. lineellus** Lec., loc. cit. 335.
3. **P. ardens** Lec., loc. cit. 334; *obscurellus* Lec. ibid. 335.
4. **P. punctulatus** Lec., ibid. 335.
5. **P. umbratus** Lec., Proc. Am. Philos. Soc. 1878, 407.
6. **P. dimissus** Lec., n. sp. ante, 35.
7. **P. collustrans** Lec., Proc. Am. Philos. Soc. 1878, 407.
8. **P. benignus** Lec., n. sp. ante, 35.
9. **P. pyralis** Linn., *(Lamp.)*, Syst. Nat. ed. xii, 644; DeGeer, iv, 52, pl. 17, f. 7;
Fabr. Syst. Ent. ii, 99; Syst. El. ii, 101; Oliv. 28, 17, pl. 2, f. 11; Lap.
Hist. Nat. Col. i, 268; Lec. loc. cit. 334; *centrata* Say, *(Lamp.)*, Journ.

---

* The locality given by Linnæus is Finland. As no species corresponding with
the description occurs in northern Europe, the name has been traditionally assigned
to our common North American species, and there seems to be no good in sub-
stituting a more recent name for that by which this species is so well known.

Acad. Nat. Sc. Phila. v, 162: ed. Lec. ii. 274: *rosata* Germ. (*Lamp.*), Ins. Nov. 62: *versicolor* ‡ Motsch. Et. Ent. 1853, 39.

10. **P. marginellus** Lec., loc. cit. 335; var. *castus* Lec. ibid. 335.
11. **P. scintillans** Say, (*Lamp.*), Journ. Acad. Nat. Sc. Phila. v, 163; ed. Lec. ii, 275; Lec. loc. cit. 335; (*Gynaptera*), List Col. N. Am. 52; Motsch. (*Macrolampis*), Et. Ent. 1853, 37.

PHAUSIS Lec.

1. **P. splendidula** Linn., (*Lamp.*), Syst. Nat. ed. xii. 644 :* Duval, (*Lamprorhiza*), Glan. Ent. i, 20; Kiesenw. Ins. Deutschl. iv. 454.
2. **P. reticulata** Say, (*Lamp.*), Journ. Acad. Nat. Sc. Phil. v, 163; ed. Lec. ii, 274: Lec. loc. cit. 337.
3. **P. inaccensa** Lec., Proc. Am. Philos. Soc. 1878, 611.

MICROPHOTUS Lec.

1. **M. dilatatus** Lec., New Sp. Col. (Smithsonian Svo.), 90.
2. **M. angustus** Lec., Trans. Am. Ent. Soc. 1874, 58.

PLEOTOMUS Lec.

1. **P. pallens** Lec., New Sp. Col. (Smithsonian Svo.), 69.
2. **P. Davisii** Lec., ante. 37.

PHOTURIS Lec.

1. **P. pensylvanica** DeGeer, (*Lamp.*), iv, 52, pl. 17, f. 8: Oliv. Ent. 28, 8, pl. 1, f. 8; Lap. (*Photinus*), Hist. Nat. i, 268; Lec. loc. cit. 337: *versicolor* Fabr. (*Lamp.*), Ent. Syst. Suppl. 123; Syst. El. ii, 105: *marginata* (*Lamp.*), Panzer, Naturforscher, xxiv, 31, pl. 1, f. 9; *lineaticollis* Motsch. (*Telephoroides*), Et. Ent. 1854, 59; *vittigera* (*Tel.*), Motsch. ibid. 60.†
2. **P. frontalis** Lec., loc. cit. 337.
3. **P. divisa** Lec., loc. cit. 337; *congener* Lec. ibid. 338.

Tribe 2.—*Phengodini.*

PTEROTUS Lec.

1. **P. obscuripennis** Lec., Pr. Ac. Nat. Sc. Phil. 1859, 86: Class. Col. N. Am. 185.

PHENGODES Illiger.

1. **P. plumosa** Oliv. (*Lamp.*), Ent. 28, 26, pl. 3, f. 27; Fabr. (*Lamp.*), Syst. ii, 105: Illiger, Mag. vi, 341; Lap. Ann. Ent. Soc. Fr. 1st. ii, 128; Hist. Nat. i, 264: Lec. loc. cit. 332; Say, Bost. Journ. Nat. Hist. i, 157; ed. Lec. ii, 634: Motsch. Et. Ent. 1854, 62.
2. **P. frontalis** Lec. ante, 39.
3. **P. laticollis** Lec. ante, 39.
4. **P. fusciceps** Lec., Class. Col. N. Am. 186.
5. **P. Sallei** Lec. ante, 39.

---

* I have given references only to the original description and to two others of recent date. The European synonymy of this introduced species need not be imported into our literature.

† The Mexican *Lamp. trilineata* Say, (Bost. Journ. Nat. Hist. i, 157; ed. Lec. ii, 634), with which Motschulsky compares this species, is evidently quite different to it in having two or three lines on each elytron yellowish.

68

J. L. LECONTE. M. D.

ZARHIPIS Lec.

1. **Z. integripennis** Lec., (*Phengodes*), Trans. Amer. Ent. Soc. 1874. 59.
2. **Z. ruficollis** Lec. ante, 39.
3. **Z. piciventris** Lec. ante, 39.

MASTINOCERUS Sol.

1. **M. texanus** Lec., Trans. Am. Ent. Soc. 1874. 59.

CENOPHENGUS Lec. n. g.

1. **C. debilis** Lec. n. sp. ante, 41.

TYTTHONYX Lec.

1. **T. erythrocephala** Fabr., (*Lamp.*), Syst. El. ii. 105; Lec. loc. cit. 347; *Malthinus serraticornis* Mels. Proc. Acad. Nat. Sc. Phila. ii, 305.

Sub-family III.— *Telephoridæ.*

CHAULIOGNATHUS Hentz.

1. **C. profundus** Lec., Proc. Acad. Nat. Sc. Phila. 1858, 71.
2. **C. disous** Lec., Proc. Acad. Nat. Sc. Phila. 1853, 230.
3. **C. fasciatus** Lec. n. sp. ante, 44.
4. **C. limbicollis** Lec., Proc. Acad. Nat. Sc. Phila. 1858, 71.
5. **C. basalis** Lec., Col. Kansas, 13, (nec Lacordaire).
6. **C. scutellaris** Lec., Proc. Acad. Nat. Sc. Phila. 1858, 230.
7. **C. Lewisii** Crotch, Trans. Amer. Ent. Soc. 1874, 78.
8. **C. opacus** Lec., N. Sp. Col. 90.
9. **C. pensylvanicus** DeGeer, Ins. iv, 78, pl. 17, f. 15: *americanus* Forster, Cent. Ins. 50; *bimaculatus* Fabr. Spec. Ins. i, 259; Lap. Hist. Nat. Col. i, 275; Oliv. Ins. &c., 26, pl. 2, f. 11.
10. **C. marginatus** Fabr., Syst. Ent. 206: Syst. El. i. 298; Lap. Hist. Nat. Col. i, 275; Hentz, Trans. Amer. Philos. Soc. iii, 460; var. *Hentzii* Lec. Proc. Acad. Nat. Sc. Phila. v, 338.

PODABRUS Westwood.

A.—*Brachynotus* Kirby.
1. **P. latimanus** Motsch., (*Malthacus*), Bull. Mosc. 1859. 402, pl. 4, f. 26; ♀ *mellifluus* Lec. Proc. Acad. Nat. Sc. Phila. 1861, 360.
2. **P. nothoides** Lec. n. sp. ante, 46.
3. **P. tricostatus** Say, Bost. Journ. Nat. Hist. i, 158; ed. Lec. ii, 236; *Bennetti* Kirby, Faun. Bor. Am. 249; *atripes* Motsch. Bull. Mosc. 1859, 403.
4. **P. rugosulus** Lec., Agass. Lake Sup. 229; Proc. Acad. Nat. Sc. Phila. v, 344.
5. **P. frater** Lec., Proc. Acad. Nat. Sc. Phila. v, 344; *quadricollis* Motsch. Bull. Mosc. 1859, 403.
6. **P. basillaris** Say, Journ. Acad. Nat. Sc. Phila. iii, 181: ed. Lec. ii, 116: *flavicollis* Lec. Proc. Acad. Nat. Sc. Phila. v, 343; *discoideus* Lec. ibid. v, 341; *punctulatus* Lec. Col. Kans. 44.
7. **P. quadratus** Lec. n. sp. ante, 46.
8. **P. fissus** Lec. n. sp. ante, 46.
9. **P. diadema** Fabr., Syst. El. i, 298; Lap. Hist. Nat. Col. i, 273; Lec. Proc. Acad. Nat. Sc. Phila. v, 344; *Malth. parvicollis* Motsch. Bull. Mosc. 1859, 402.

10. **P. modestus** Say, Journ. Acad. Nat. Sc. Phila. iii, 179; ed. Lec. ii, 117.
11. **P. binotatus** Lec. n. sp. ante. 47.
12. **P. comes** Lec., Proc. Acad. Nat. Sc. Phila. v, 344; *torquatus* Lec. ibid. 1861, 350: *gradatus* Lec. ibid. 1860, 320.
13. **P. tomentosus** Say, Journ. Acad. Nat. Sc. Phila. v, 165; ed. Lec. 276; *rufiolus* Mels. Proc. Acad. ii, 304; *pruinosus* Lec. ibid. v, 344; *cinercipennis* Motsch. B. M. 1859, 403.
14. **P. protensus** Lec., N. Sp. Col. 91; *Fayi* Lec. ibid. 91.
15. **P. brunnicollis** Fabr., (*Canth.*), Sp. Ins. i, 258; Syst. El. i, 298; Lec. Proc. Acad. Nat. Sc. Phila. v, 345; *Canth. limbatus* Fabr. Sp. Ins. i, 258;' var. *puncticollis* ǁ Lec. Proc. Acad. Nat. Sc. Phila. v, 345; *poricollis* Lec. ibid. 1852, 49.

B.—*Malthacus* Kirby.
16. **P. scaber** Lec., Proc. Acad. Nat. Sc. Phila. 1861, 350.
17. **P. cinctipennis** Lec., N. Sp. Col. 91.
18. **P. limbellus** Lec. n. sp. ante, 47.
19. **P. punctatus** Lec., Agass. Lake Sup. 229.
20. **P. brevipennis** Lec., Bull. U. S. Geol. Surv. 1878. iv, 460.
21. **P. puncticollis** Kby., Faun. Bor. Am. 247; *marginellus* Lec. Agass. Lake Sup. 229.
22. **P. xanthoderus** Lec. n. sp. ante, 48.
23. **P. lutosus** Lec. n. sp. ante, 48.
24. **P. macer** Lec., Proc. Acad. Nat. Sc. Phila. 1861, 350.
25. **P. piniphilus** Esch., Bull. Mosc. 1830, 65; Mann. ibid. 1843, 246.
26. **P. lateralis** Lec., Annual Rept. Ch. Eng. U. S. Army, 1876, 297.
27. **P. puberulus** Lec., Agass. Lake Sup. 227; ? *sericatus* Mann. Bull. Mosc. 1846, 511.
28. **P. extremus** Lec. n. sp. ante, 48.
29. **P. simplex** Couper. Can. Nat. 1865, 62.
30. **P. lævicollis** Kirby, Faun. Bor. Am. 248.
31. **P. tejonicus** Lec., Proc. Acad. Nat. Sc. Phila. 1859, 74.
32. **P. Bolteri** Lec. n. sp. ante, 49.
33. **P. Pattoni** Lec., Proc. Acad. Nat. Sc. Phila. 1866, 394.

C.
34. **P. mellitus** Lec. n. sp. ante, 49.
35. **P. corneus** Lec., Proc. Acad. Nat. Sc. 1861, 350.
36. **P. cavicollis** Lec. ibid. 1851, 345.

TELEPHORUS DeGeer.
A.
1. **T. dentiger** Lec., Proc. Acad. Nat. Sc. Phila. v, 341.
2. **T. excavatus** Lec. ibid. v, 342.
3. **T. vilis** Lec. ibid. v, 343.
4. **T. tantillus** Lec. n. sp.; *pusio* ǁ Lec. ante, 51.
5. **T. Walshii** Lec. n. sp. ante, 51.
6. **T. fraxini** Say, Journ. Acad. Nat. Sc. Phila. iii, 181; ed. Lec. ii, 118; Lec. Proc. Acad. v, 343; *ater* Kirby, Faun. Bor. Am. 245; *Rhag. binodula* Mann. Bull. Mosc. 1846, 512; *nigrita* Lec. Agass. Lake Sup. 229.

B.

7. **T. carolinus** Fabr., Syst. El. i, 296; var. *jactatus* Say, Journ. Acad. Nat. Sc.
Phila. v, 167; ed. Lec. ii, 277.
8. **T. lineola** Fabr., Ent. Syst. i, 219; Syst. El. i, 301; Coq. Ill. Ins. iii, 127, pl. 29,
f. 1; *C. parallela* Say, Journ. Acad. Nat. Sc. Phila. v, 168; ed. Lec. ii,
277; *Sayi* Lec. Proc. Acad. v, 342.
9. **T. nigritulus** Lec. n. sp. ante, 52.
10. **T. rectus** Mels., Proc. Acad. Nat. Sc. Phila. ii, 305; Lec. ibid. v, 342; *pusillus*
Lec. ibid. v, 343; *oriflavus* Lec. Proc. Bost. Soc. Nat. Hist. 1874, 273.
11. **T. nanulus** Lec. n. sp. ante, 52.
12. **T. cruralis** Lec. Proc. Acad. Nat. Sc. Phila. v, 342.
13. **T. flavipes** Lec. ibid. v, 341; ? var. *dichrous* Lec. ibid. v, 341.
14. **T. scitulus** Say, Journ. Acad. Nat. Sc. Phila. v, 168; ed. Lec. ii, 278; *imbecillis*
Lec. Proc. Acad. v, 342; *nigriceps* Lec. Agass. Lake Sup. 230.
15. **T. pusillus** Lec. Proc. Acad. Nat. Sc. Phila. v, 343.
16. **T. luteicollis** Germ., Ins. Nov. 70; *cinetellus* Lec. Proc. Acad. Nat. Sc. Phila.
v, 341.
17. **T. ruficollis** Lec. n. sp. ante, 53.
18. **T. longulus** Lec. Proc. Acad. Nat. Sc. Phila. v, 343.

C.

19. **T. impar** Lec. n. sp. ante, 53.

D.

20. **T. consors** Lec., Proc. Acad. Nat. Sc. Phila. v, 340; ♀ *tibialis* ‖ Lec. ibid. v, 340;
tibiellus Gemm., Ent. Hefte vi, 1876, (nomen superfl.).
21. **T. rotundicollis** Say, Journ. Acad. Nat. Sc. Phila. v, 165.
22. **T. Curtisii** Kirby, Faun. Bor. Am. 247; *Samouelli* Kirby, ibid. 246.
23. **T. transmarinus** Motsch., Bull. Mosc. 1859, 400.
24. **T. grandicollis** Lec., Proc. Acad. Nat. Sc. Phila. v, 340; = *rubricollis* Motsch.
Bull. Mosc. 1859, 400.
25. **T. fidelis** Lec. ibid. v, 340.
26. **T. oregonus** Lec., New Sp. 92; *scopus* Lec. ibid. 92.
27. **T. tuberculatus** Lec., Proc. Acad. Nat. Sc. Phila. v, 341; *impressus* Lec. ibid.
v, 341; ♀ *brevicollis* Lec. ibid. v, 341; var. *collaris* ‖ Lec. ibid. 340;
armiger Couper, Can. Nat. 1865, 62.
28. **T. alticola** Lec. n. sp. ante, 54.
29. **T. bilineatus** Say, Journ. Acad. Nat. Sc. Phila. iii, 182.

E.

30. **T. divisus** Lec., Proc. Acad. Nat. Sc. Phila. v, 340; *latinsculus* Motsch. Bull.
Mosc. 1859, 401, pl. iv, f. 25.
31. **T. notatus** Mann., Bull. Mosc. 1843, 246; *peregrinus* Boh. Eugen. Resa, 80;
var. *larvalis* Lec. Pacific R.R. Report, 48.
32. **T. lautus** Lec., Proc. Acad. Nat. Sc. Phila. v, 340.
33. **T. ochropus** Lec. n. sp. ante, 54.

F.

34. **T. ingenuus** Lec. n. sp. ante, 55.

G.

35. **T. marginellus** Lec., Proc. Acad. Nat. Sc. Phila. v, 342.

POLEMIUS Lec.

1. **P. platyderus** Gemm., Col. Hefte, 1870 ; *planicollis* ‖ Lec. Journ. Acad. Nat. Sc. Phila. 1858, 17.
2. **P. laticornis** Say, Journ. Acad. Nat. Sc. Phila. v, 168 ; *T. dubius* Mels. Proc. Acad. Nat. Sc. Phila. ii, 304 ; var. *incisus* Lec. ibid. v, 168.
3. **P. repandus** Lec. n. sp. ante, 55.
4. **P. limbatus** Lec., Proc. Acad. Nat. Sc. Phila. v, 339.

SILIS Charp.

1. **S. spinigera** Lec., Trans. Amer. Ent. Soc. 1874, 61.
2. **S. munita** Lec. n. sp. ante, 56.
3. **S. difficilis** Lec., Proc. Acad. Nat. Sc. Phila. v, 230.
4. **S. flavida** Lec., Trans. Amer. Ent. Soc. 1874, 61.
5. **S. cava** Lec. ibid. 1874, 61.
6. **S. pallida** Mann., Bull. Mosc. 1843, 246.
7. **S. percomis** Say, Bost. Journ. Nat. Hist. i, 159 ; ed. Lec. ii, 637 ; ♂ *longicornis* Lec. Agass. Lake Sup. 230 ; ♀ *Telephorus curtus* Lec. ibid. 231.
8. **S. vulnerata** Lec., Trans. Am. Ent. Soc. 1874, 61.
9. **S. lutea** Lec., Journ. Acad. Nat. Sc. Phila. 2d. v, 333 ; *pallens* ‖ Lec. Proc. Acad. Nat. Sc. Phila. v, 339.
10. **S. filigera** Lec., Trans. Am. Ent. Soc. 1874, 62.
11. **S. spathulata** Lec. n. sp. ante, 57.
12. **S. perforata** Lec. n. sp. ante, 57.

DITEMNUS Lec.

1. **D. bidentatus** Say, Journ. Acad. Nat. Sc. Phila. v, 169 ; ed. Lec. ii, 278 ; Lec. Proc. Acad. Nat. Sc. Phila. v, 339.
2. **D. obtusus** Lec., Trans. Am. Philos. Soc. 1874, 62.
3. **D. fossiger** n. sp. ante, 58.

TRYPHERUS Lec.

1. **T. latipennis** Germ. Ins. Nov. 72 ; Lap. Hist. Nat. i, 277 ; Lec. Proc. Acad. Nat. Sc. Phila. v, 346 ; *Lygerus lat.* Kiesenw. Linn. Ent. vii, 246 ; *Molorchus marginalis* Say, Long's Exp. ii, 192 ; ed. Lec. i, 293.

LOBETUS Kiesenw.

1. **L. abdominalis** Lec., Proc. Acad. Nat. Sc. Phila. v, 347.

MALTHINUS Latr.

1. **M. atripennis** n. sp. ante, 60.
2. **M occipitalis** Lec., Proc. Acad. Nat. Sc. Phila. v, 345 ; *difficilis* Lec. ibid. v, 345.

MALTHODES Kiesenw.

A.

1. **M. spado** Lec., N. Sp. Col. 93.

B.

2. **M. laticollis** Lec., List Col. N. Am. 53 ; *transversus* ‖ Lec. Proc. Acad. Nat. Sc. Phila. 1861, 351.
3. **M. concavus** Lec., Proc. Acad. Nat. Sc. Phila. v, 346.

C.

4. **M. fragilis** Lec., Pr. Ac. Nat. Sc. Phil. v. 346 = *transversus* Lec. ibid. v, 346.
I have taken advantage of this synonymy to suppress the latter specific name as more likely to produce confusion.
5. **M. exilis** Mels. ibid. ii. 305.
6. **M. fusculus** Lec. ibid. v, 346.
7. **M. rectus** n. sp. ante, 61.
8. **M. curvatus** n. sp. ante, 61.
9. **M. furcifer** n. sp. ante, 62.
10. **M. arcifer** n. sp. ante, 62.
11. **M. captiosus** n. sp. ante, 61.
12. **M. fuliginosus** Lec., N. Sp. Col. 93.
13. **M. niger** Lec., Proc. Acad. Nat. Sc. Phila. v. 346.

Unclassified females.

14. **M. analis** n. sp. ante, 62.
15. **M. congruus** n. sp. ante, 62.
16. **M. quadricollis** n. sp. ante, 63.
17. **M. parvulus** Lec., Proc. Acad. Nat. Sc. Phila. v, 346.

Undetermined species.

Luciola maculicollis Lap. Ann. Ent. Soc. Fr. ii, 148. This genus does not occur in America.
Cantharis vittata Fabr. Ent. Syst. i, 219.
Cantharis rufipes Say, Journ. Acad. Nat. Sc. Phila. iii, 182; ed. Lec. ii, 118. The form of the claws not being given, this name may be referred to several species of *Telephorus*.
Cantharodema marginipennis Lap. Hist. Nat. Col. i. 276.
Malthodes ruficollis Kiesenwetter, Linn. Ent. vii, 320.

In concluding this paper, I have only to regret, that although, several of my friends, who have collaborated with me, for the procuring of material to render it as perfect as possible, the position and affinities of the tribe Phengodini must still remain uncertain, in consequence of the ignorance in which we remain in regard to the habits of the species, and the form of the females. It may be inferred from the observations of Mrs. King on the larva and male imago of *Mastinocerus* that they are luminous in all stages of development. This inference must, however, be confirmed by those who have the opportunity of observing in a living condition the genera and species of the tribe, which as will be seen in the foregoing pages are widely distributed. The male of *Pterotus*, as I have been recently informed by Mr. Rivers, flies in the evening twilight, but I have not yet learned if it has any luminous power.

www.ingramcontent.com/pod-product-compliance
Lightning Source LLC
Chambersburg PA
CBHW021637270326
41931CB00008B/1062